Alison - I Love You!

Presented To

FeeFee

From

Christmas 2018

Date

Psa 37:4

Praise for
Desires of Your Heart

"Michael has a gift and writes from his heart. He is a true man of God and his words have touched many lives. He sees the beauty in others and shares his life experiences, insights and feelings with honesty and love."- *Nancy from Illinois*

"......his poems have touched my heart.......the poems this gifted man writes are a true inspiration to us all. Michael brings our Heavenly Father's guidance and words of scripture in layman's terms." - *Melody from Texas*

"Your poems saved me Michael; they touched my heart and gave me Peace, the kind that surpasses all understanding. And then you would arm me with the written word and those scriptures became my armor and my shield and soon, I wasn't so sad or discouraged or even ashamed. I'm proud to be a child of God, a horse lover, a cowgirl with those old fashioned morals."- *Maura from Arizona*

"Desires of Your Heart will help you open your heart to hear God speak to you day by day. Your spirit will overflow, as you are embraced by the One who loves you more than you can imagine."- *Debra from Kansas*

DESIRES
OF YOUR
HEART

Stories of Life Written in Rhyme

MICHAEL GASAWAY

Published by Diamond G Publishing.

Cover painting by Denny Karchner
The cover painting is available for sale. Contact Denny at his web site for more information on this or other western art. **www.karchnerwesternart.com**

Graphic design, front and back cover art by Denny Karchner

ISBN-13: 978-0692516737

Printed in USA

This book is dedicated to my family, friends, and anyone who has journeyed down "Life's Highway" in search of your dream. To my sons of whom I'm so proud of the men you have become. To my youngest son Sammy who now inspires us all from heaven above. "Time to go climb that mountain again, Sammy. See you at the top!"

I hope these poems put a smile on your face, a song in your heart or maybe a tear in your eye when you remember back to that first hello or last goodbye. Remember you're never too young or too old to seek out and follow your dreams.
God Bless, Never Give Up and Keep Dreamin'.

Thank you to my many Facebook followers who have taken this journey in rhyme with me. Your comments have been very motivational and kept me writing when I was wondering if it was doing any good.

Follow me on Facebook at:
https://www.facebook.com/michaelthepoetryman.

Thank you everyone who has offered suggestions for poems. I hope you see a story written in rhyme within these pages that bring you inspiration, faith and peace.

I would also like to thank Denny Karchner for his time and efforts in producing the graphic art work and cover painting for the book.

Thank you to my Mom and my brother Mark, for your assistance in bringing this book to realization.

Thank you God for guiding my pen that wrote these words. Thank you God for providing me with the inspiration that has touched so many hearts and changed so many lives.

Guide to Story Themes

Attitude: 22, 70, 72, 74, 88, 102, 104, 108, 118, 122, 130, 132, 134, 140, 146

Adversity: 16, 32, 58, 60, 70, 72, 74, 76, 78, 86, 88, 94, 98, 102, 104, 106, 118, 122

Believe: 8, 10, 22, 34, 42, 44, 48, 52, 62, 64, 68, 72, 76, 86, 98, 104, 116, 136, 140, 146

Brokenness: 62, 64, 66, 82, 88, 94, 102, 108

Desires: 8, 12, 24, 26, 30, 32, 34, 36, 38, 42, 48, 80, 98, 136, 140, 146

Destiny: 8, 12, 14, 30, 32, 34, 36, 38, 42, 52, 60, 68, 72, 140

Dreams: 12, 24, 28, 30, 34, 36, 38, 48, 52, 82, 114, 120, 138, 146

Change: 10, 22, 34, 36, 74, 94, 96, 1023, 126

Choices: 8, 10, 16, 34, 36, 38, 46, 54, 60, 62, 64, 66, 70, 84, 108, 112, 118, 122, 124, 126, 128, 132, 136

Communication: 54, 112, 122, 124, 130, 132, 134

Faith: 8, 10, 16, 20, 28, 32, 40, 42, 52, 58, 68, 72, 78, 82, 90, 92, 98, 100, 104, 106, 110, 126, 136, 138, 140

Fear: 10, 16, 50, 70, 84, 96, 114, 118, 120, 136

Hope: 8, 18, 52, 64, 80, 84, 98, 102, 106, 110, 116, 140, 146

Honesty: 122, 124, 126, 130, 132, 136

Loss: 42, 44, 46, 72, 74, 78, 80, 88, 94, 122, 138

Love: 10, 14, 18, 20, 26, 28, 30, 32, 44, 46, 48, 50, 56, 58, 80, 84, 110, 112, 114, 116, 118, 122, 124, 132, 140

Music: 24, 26, 28, 34, 36

Pain: 46, 56, 60, 72, 76, 78, 84, 88, 122, 138

Passion: 12, 14, 20, 24, 26, 28, 30, 34, 36, 114

Purpose: 8, 54, 94, 96

Sorrow: 52, 62, 74, 78, 122, 138

Stress: 52, 66, 70, 76, 100, 104

Temptation: 16, 74, 84, 86, 94, 128

Trials: 10, 54, 64, 66, 68, 88, 102, 122, 124, 138

Trust: 20, 40, 42, 44, 56, 68, 74, 76, 82, 86, 100, 104, 106, 120, 128, 136, 138, 140, 146

Worry: 70, 76, 82, 88, 92, 100, 112, 118, 120, 136

Table of Contents in Alphabetical Order

Michael Gasaway

Follow Your Dreams

Another year around the sun;
Now it's time to finish what you've left undone.

It's never too late to begin anew;
To follow those dreams you still carry within you.

We all have dreams left unfinished we carry deep inside;
Don't carry them with you, when you die.

Live each day to the fullest and make it the best one yet;
Let no day finish, with any regret.

Saddle up each day and grab hold of life's reins;
Leave behind all your past worries and life's many strains.

Ride into the future intending to make your dreams come true;
Beyond the horizon they're waiting for you.

God made you special with certain gifts inside;
How, when and if you use them, you get to decide.

So decide today to again follow your dreams;
No matter how far or difficult they may seem.

You're never too old or young to start;
Just always do what's right and follow your heart.

Then one day with a smile on your face;
You'll realize, one dream is finished and a new one to chase.

As long as you have a new dream in your heart;
Then each day will always bring forth a fresh new start.

It's a circle of life and dreams you follow each day;
Achieving each, teaches you a new lesson along life's highway.

No time to waste, start today to follow your dreams;
They may really be a lot closer than it seems.

Say a prayer to God up above;
That He will lead and guide you always, with His merciful
love.

I pray that you'll discover your true purpose in life along the way;
And that all your dreams, you'll realize one day.

~~~

"In his grace, God has given us different gifts for doing certain things well......."
Romans 12:6

Delight yourself in the Lord, and he will give you the desires of your heart.
Psalm 37:4

Commit your way to the Lord; trust in him, and he will act.
Psalm 37:5

For where your treasure is, there your heart will be also.
Matthew 6:21

The plans of the heart belong to man, but the answer of the tongue is from the Lord. All the ways of a man are pure in   his own eyes, but the Lord weighs the spirit. Commit your work to the Lord, and your plans will be established.
Proverbs 16:1-3

The heart of man plans his way, but the Lord establishes his steps.
Proverbs 16:9

For still the vision awaits its appointed time; it hastens to the end—it will not lie. If it seems slow, wait for it; it will surely come; it will not delay.
Habakkuk 2:3

Michael Gasaway

Worthy of Love

She had come full circle from where she had begun;
Now she just looked to the west, and the setting sun.

Sometimes she questioned her self-worth when it came to love;
It was at these troubled times she asked why, to God above.

Was she truly worthy of love she asked herself at this time;
This was the thought that now crossed the caverns of her mind.

Her thoughts took her back in time and she thought of him;
At times she wondered if she could ever be loved like that again.

The questions came flashing across her mind like rays of the
sunset;
Had she let true love slip by, while playing love's roulette?

Your self-worth is your decision to make alone;
Belief in yourself has to be the foundation and your cornerstone.

You must truly feel worthy of love to find it one day;
Don't be too quick to give up and just walk away.

Believe in yourself and all that God has created you to be;
Let go and let God, guide you to your destiny.

Tell yourself that you deserve the best and are truly worthy of
love;
Then pray that God will guide your steps from up above.

Your self-worth is comprised by the way that you think;
Change is up to you, but belief in yourself is the link.

So go forward with your head held high;
Believe in yourself and in true love, and to your fears, say
goodbye.

~~~

In all thy ways acknowledge him, and he shall direct thy paths.
Proverbs 3:6

For God gave us a spirit not of fear but of power and love and self-control.
2 Timothy 1:7

For you formed my inward parts; you knitted me together in my mother's womb. I praise you, for I am fearfully and wonderfully made. Wonderful are your works; my soul knows it very well. My frame was not hidden from you, when I was being made in secret, intricately woven in the depths of the earth.
Psalm 139:13-15

For I know the plans I have for you, declares the Lord, plans for welfare and not for evil, to give you a future and a hope. Jeremiah 29:11

Love suffers long and is kind; love does not envy; love does not parade itself, is not puffed up; does not behave rudely, does not seek its own, is not provoked, thinks no evil; does not rejoice in iniquity, but rejoices in the truth; bears all things, believes all things, hopes all things, endures all things. Love never fails. 1 Corinthians 13:4-8

Ask, and it will be given to you; seek, and you will find; knock, and it will be opened to you.
Matthew 7:7

Let all that you do be done in love.
1 Corinthians 16:14

Michael Gasaway

"COWGIRL"

"Horse lover", "roper" or "barrel racer", all of these and more she
has been called;
But "Cowgirl" is the term she likes best of all.

It describes her right down to a tee you see;
From her earliest childhood memories, it is what she's always
wanted to be.

From her Stetson down to her boots n' spurs, oh how she looks
the part;
But her real cowgirl spirit lies deep within her heart.

You see being a cowgirl is not just about how she may dress and
talk;
A real cowgirl not only talks the talk but she walks the walk.

"Cowgirl" is an attitude that comes from deep in her heart within;
To her it is a way of living life from the beginning to the very
end.

She can be tough and gentle, sexy and wild, sweet and kind;
Sometimes you'll swear that she has just plum lost her mind.

For a cowgirl has a mind of her own you see;
It will most often be a mystery and just seems to confound you
and me.

So never try to change her or fence her in;
If you ever make her a promise, you'd better keep it my friend.

As she may not remember it, but she will never forget;
And in the end, may leave you with heart ache and regret.

She may have the charms of a southern belle;
But when the time comes, she can be hard as nails.

From cleaning stalls to riding all day;
When this cowgirl dresses up for a night with her man, she
will leave him breathless with nothing to say.

She doesn't need a man to make her feel right;
But she sure does miss one, on some of those cold and lonesome nights.

Alone with just her dog and horse she'd rather stay;
Than to live with a man who doesn't understand her cowgirl ways.

In her mind it's not too hard to comprehend;
She just wants a man to love her unconditionally, and be her best and trusted friend.

A friend and lover by both night and day;
And to always stand by her side no matter what life may throw their way.

Yes, a cowgirl is a very special woman in this world of strife;
And if you're lucky enough to find one, hang on to her as you're in for the ride of your life.

Thank God for all you cowgirls out there don't ever change your ways;
Sit deep in the saddle, grab hold of life's reins and be proud of being a "COWGIRL" each and every day.

∿∿∿

And let us not grow weary of doing good, for in due season we will reap, if we do not give up. Galatians 6:9

Charm is deceitful, and beauty is vain, but a woman who fears the Lord is to be praised. Proverbs 31:30

Make no friendship with a man given to anger, nor go with a wrathful man, lest you learn his ways and entangle yourself in a snare .Proverbs 22:24-25

Delight yourself in the Lord, and he will give you the desires of your heart. Psalm 37:4

Michael Gasaway

The Cowboy and the Lady

A cowboy was he from his Stetson hat to his custom ostrich
boots;
She had a Michael Kors purse and elegant fashion in her roots.

Grand Ole Opry and Texas red dirt music was his musical choice;
The Metropolitan Opera and the symphony to her, gave music its
voice.

From different worlds they came together on that fateful night;
That's sometimes how it happens, when God lets love take flight.

He had started to stir dormant emotions deep inside her heart
and soul;
For one of the few times in her life, she was beginning to feel out
of control.

What was happening to her as all the feelings started to flash
across her mind?
It all seemed to happen so fast and in such a short period of
time.

This cowboy had first touched her with the sweet words he had
written;
Then she heard his voice, and knew then, that she was smitten.

Their first kiss together had them both seeing stars and wanting
more;
They both felt a connection between them that neither had ever
felt before.

So rugged and tough, but yet his touch was so soft and gentle it
seemed;
The days with him seemed to unfold as out of some romantic
dream.

Now she wondered how their story would in time unfold;
She didn't realize then, but it was her story to be told.

Yes a Cowboy and a Lady came together on that star filled
Texas night;
Now the years have gone by and she knew it had been right.

Sometimes things happen we don't seem to understand;
So it is when it comes to this special love between a woman
and a man.

It never makes sense at first glance as we see it begin;
Then one day it all comes together and true love prevails in the
end.

Never underestimate the power of love or how it may find you;
Sometimes it comes like a bolt of lightning as it did for these
two.

So be patient, never give up on love and always be aware;
Tonight for star struck lovers everywhere, let's all lift up a
prayer.

~~~

And now these three remain: faith, hope and love. But the
greatest of these is love.
1 Corinthians 13:13

Let all that you do be done in love.
1 Corinthians 16:14

And above all these put on love, which binds everything together
in perfect harmony.
Colossians 3:14

Beloved, let us love one another, for love is from God, and
whoever loves has been born of God and knows God.
1 John 4:7

There is no fear in love, but perfect love casts out fear. For
fear has to do with punishment, and whoever fears has not been
perfected in love.
1 John 4:18

Michael Gasaway

"Good Ride, Cowboy...Good Ride"

Life is a lot like a rodeo some ole cowboys say;
You nod your head, the gate opens and you're on your way.

As in life, you never know what bronc you may draw;
You just cowboy up each time and give it your all.

You never know which way the 'bronc' may turn;
But with every move it makes, another life lesson you learn.

You just have to hang on tight, and dig your spurs in;
You know in your heart, now's not the time to think about
quittin'.

Like the devil he will try to throw you to the ground;
But you know if you hang on, you'll hear that 8 second buzzer
sound.

He'll try every trick that he can to throw you to the side;
Just hang on to life's reins and enjoy the ride.

Like life you never know how the ride might end;
This could be the time that the gold buckle you finally win.

The ride sometimes seems to go on forever as you're jerked all
about;
You know that now's not the time to have any self doubt.

Somewhere in the distance you hear the crowd start to cheer;
It's like a heavenly sound in your ear, and you know the end of
the ride is almost here.

The buzzer sounds and your ride is at its end;
The *pickup-man* is there to greet you just like a trusted friend.

Yes, life is a lot like a rodeo; those ole cowboys had some
great insight;
You just have to hang on and enjoy the ride and always do
what's right.

So when your ride is over and you breathe your last sigh;
Then you will hear in the distance God say,
"Good Ride Cowboy...Good Ride".

~~~

Delight yourself in the Lord, and he will give you the desires of your heart.
Psalm 37:4

Trust in the Lord with all your heart, and do not lean on your own understanding.
Proverbs 3:5

Now faith is the assurance of things hoped for, the conviction of things not seen.
Hebrews 11:1

For I know the plans I have for you, declares the Lord,   plans for welfare and not for evil, to give you a future and a hope.
Jeremiah 29:11

For God gave us a spirit not of fear but of power and love and self-control.
2 Timothy 1:7

For still the vision awaits its appointed time; it hastens to the end—it will not lie. If it seems slow, wait for it; it will surely come; it will not delay.
Habakkuk 2:3

Michael Gasaway

Desert Ride

Across the desert they rode with only the moon and stars lighting
their way;
On they rode to that special spot where they could watch the
dawning of a new day.

Placing a blanket on the ground and opening some wine for them
to share;
They sat together watching the heavens above, each without a
care.

Watching the stars while sipping wine, they talked of many
things;
The past, the present and what tomorrow may bring.

Holding each other tightly, they watched the stars shoot across
the desert sky;
Inside each could feel the beginning of love, and saw it in each
other's eyes.

The night went on and they toasted one another with each sip of
wine they drank;
Time slipped by too quickly for them, as the full moon slowly
sank.

Sinking into the desert sand as the sun was rising to begin its
daily quest;
It was a special time for each of them, a special memory, for
each the best.

In the early morning light, back across the desert they rode side
by side;
Each was smiling at the other remembering, the beautiful moonlit
ride.

Was this the beginning of something special each was thinking
as they rode?
Back across the desert, each was wondering how this love story
would unfold.

~~~

Let all that you do be done in love.
1 Corinthians 16:14

And above all these put on love, which binds everything together in perfect harmony.
Colossians 3:14

There is no fear in love, but perfect love casts out fear. For fear has to do with punishment, and whoever fears has not been perfected in love.
1 John 4:18

Let love be genuine. Abhor what is evil; hold fast to what is good. Romans 12:9

Delight yourself in the Lord, and he will give you the desires of your heart.
Psalm 37:4

With all humility and gentleness, with patience, bearing with one another in love,
Ephesians 4:2

Delight yourself in the Lord, and he will give you the desires of your heart.
Psalm 37:4

Michael Gasaway

Autumn Trail

The best, oh yes the very best is yet to be;
Come now My Love and take this journey with me.

Let us journey far and wide so that everyone will see;
Our magical trip of love and devotion, together always we'll be.

Together in love we will travel as one down life's road.
Yes my love, come now so that soon we may go.

God brought us together in part to show others there is hope;
To help show them God's way and sometimes how to cope.

Such an inspiration we will be, as others see the love we project;
First comes our love of God in our lives and then for each other,
as He directs.

This is a love so pure and true directed from God on high;
Together we'll ride down the autumn trail, side by side.

Yes this is a true story of a love that is so very real;
It happened one autumn day, when their hearts again began to
feel.

They both had put their trust in God above and kept their faith in
Him;
Now together they ride into this new beautiful life, ready to begin
again.

So never give up and keep your trust and faith in God above;
He answers all prayers in His time, even prayers to find true love.

~~~

And let us not grow weary of doing good, for in due season we will reap, if we do not give up.
Galatians 6:9

Let all that you do be done in love.
1 Corinthians 16:14

And above all these put on love, which binds everything together in perfect harmony.
Colossians 3:14

With all humility and gentleness, with patience, bearing with one another in love,
Ephesians 4:2

Love is patient and kind; love does not envy or boast; it is not arrogant or rude. It does not insist on its own way; it is not irritable or resentful; it does not rejoice at wrongdoing, but rejoices with the truth. Love bears all things, believes all things, hopes all things, endures all things.
1 Corinthians 13:4-7

Michael Gasaway

Cactus Rose

Even among the thorns of life there is beauty to be seen;
Just open up your eyes and behold God's amazing scenes.

At times what we see is desolation all around;
In an instant can change and suddenly with the light of day,
beauty abounds.

Some people see only the thorns and dried up ground for miles
and miles;
Others see only the beauty, and to them, it brings a smile.

Beauty is all around us if we just open up our eyes to see;
Sometime all it takes, is for you to just really believe.

You can see the thorns and the harshness of life each day;
Or you can see the beauty of a cactus rose on display.

Each stage of life brings to us a different view;
Sometimes what you see is that which is really inside of you.

So try to see the beauty and good in each day;
Start each day by taking time to pray.

Then pray that God will open your eyes to see the beauty all
around;
Even in the cactus rose, blooming forth from hard scrabbled
ground.

~~~

And God saw everything that he had made, and behold, it was very good. And there was evening and there was morning, the sixth day.
Genesis 1:31

And whatever you ask in prayer, you will receive, if you have faith.
Matthew 21:22

Not that I am speaking of being in need, for I have learned in whatever situation I am to be content.
Philippians 4:11

Arise, shine, for your light has come, and the glory of the Lord has risen upon you.
Isaiah 60:1

Casting all your anxieties on him, because he cares for you.
1 Peter 5:7

Michael Gasaway

Current of Desire

They sing and write the songs and rhymes for you and me;
Inspiration comes from their hearts and at times on a summer
breeze.

Playing, writing and singing of love, both lost and found;
Of how two people must first find good common ground.

Some poems and songs take us deep within their very soul;
While others are written just to let someone out there know.

No matter the music, prose or rhymes that they may sing or
write;
Each and everyone will touch you, showing such great insight.

Their rhymes and music are but a current of desire;
That's flowing just beneath the surface, coming forth to inspire.

They'll take you to places you have never been before;
And tantalize you with their words and music in a soft and
seductive lore.

One of a kind are these special women of music, rhyme and
song;
If you're lucky enough to meet one, you'd better hang on.

Truth be known, they are a unique brand of woman you see;
Very loving, sweet and tender are they, yet very much a
mystery.

They can be soft, sexy, sensuous, wild, gentle and kind;
Special are these women that can drive you right out of your
mind.

Beauty, poise, grace and intelligence with such a seductive way;

Most men will be left in their wake with little or nothing left to
say.

Treat these remarkable women with care and never do one
wrong;
Cause if you're not careful, you could end up in a poem or
song.

God Bless to all you cowgirl singers/song writers and poets of
time;
Keep writing and singing, inspiring us all with every song,
word and rhyme.

∿∿∿

*The Lord announces the word, and the women who proclaim it
are a mighty throng:*
Psalm 68:11

*My heart, O God, is steadfast; I will sing and make music with
all my soul.*
Psalm 108:1

*Gracious words are a honeycomb, sweet to the soul and healing
to the bones.*
Proverbs 16:24

*A Psalm for giving thanks. Make a joyful noise to the Lord, all
the earth! Serve the Lord with gladness! Come into his presence
with singing!*
Psalm 100:1-2

*I will sing to the Lord as long as I live; I will sing praise to my
God while I have being.*
Psalm 104:33

*Whoever sings songs to a heavy heart is like one who takes off
a garment on a cold day, and like vinegar on soda.*
Proverbs 25:20

*Sing praises to the Lord with the lyre, with the lyre and the
sound of melody!*
Psalm 98:5

Michael Gasaway

The Music Girl

Oh how her music does make our hearts and souls sing;
Playing her music is one of her favorite things.

She plays the flute, piano and cello too;
Hearing her music can lift you up when you're feeling blue.

Listening to her music can brighten even the darkest of days;
Listen as she plays sweet music up on that stage.

How her green eyes do sparkle in the light;
It's her music that will fill your heart with such delight.

So alive inside with God's peace and joy is she;
When along with the orchestra, she plays such a sweet melody.

A very talented and beautiful lady fair this is true;
Playing music at church is by far her favorite venue.

Her talent she knows that is a gift from God above;
That's why she plays it with such devotion and love.

The dark and the hard times she has seen plenty of;
But she got through them with her music and God's love.

Passing on her gift and love of music to those she does teach;
Oh the many young hearts she has been able to reach.

How alive, the music does make her soul feel deep inside;
Playing a special song fills her heart and soul with such pride.

Always she plays the songs with such love and devotion;
It is to God in Heaven above that she gives her adoration.

God bless her and all those that play the instruments and do
sing;
It's their music our hearts hear, that satisfies our souls longing.

~~~

26

My heart, O God, is steadfast; I will sing and make music with all my soul.
Psalm 108:1

Oh come, let us sing to the Lord; let us make a joyful noise to the rock of our salvation!
Psalm 95:1

The Lord announces the word, and the women who proclaim it are a mighty throng:
Psalm 68:11

Addressing one another in psalms and hymns and spiritual songs, singing and making melody to the Lord with your heart,
Ephesians 5:19

Sing praises to the Lord with the lyre, with the lyre and the sound of melody!
Psalm 98:5

They sing to the tambourine and the lyre and rejoice to the sound of the pipe.
Job 21:12

Praise him with tambourine and dance; praise him with strings and pipe!
Psalm 150:4

Michael Gasaway

Passion and Dreams

Horses and music are her passion, that is so plain to see;
Feeling the wind on her face is her favorite places to be.

Making music and horses are what she really loves the best;
Unlike most people, a horse will always pass her test.

They are special creatures this she knows in her heart;
It is with horses she will always want to be a part.

Her blue eyes, oh how they do sparkle and glow;
When across the hills riding her horse she does go.

See how her blond hair gently blows in the wind,
On she will ride until daylight fades, and night time does begin.

Yes, Horses and playing music are her passion it seems;
She knows that they will always be a part of her dreams.

As she rides, God paints another spectacular sunset across the
Texas sky;
In her heart she knows that with him soon, she will one day ride.

Off they will ride into the setting sun is how she sees it in her
mind;
How often she had dreamed of it, time after time.

One day soon her dream will come true, of finding that one
special love;
Together always, side by side they will ride, blessed from God
above.

Never give up on your dreams, especially those of love and your
passion;
Keep praying and believing as one day, they will become your
realization.

God put dreams, passions and talents into us all for a special
reason;
Keep yours alive by believing and get ready for your harvest
season.

~~~

And we know that for those who love God all things work together for good, for those who are called according to his purpose.
Romans 8:28

Delight yourself in the Lord, and he will give you the desires of your heart.
Psalm 37:4

I will instruct you and teach you in the way you should go; I will counsel you with my eye upon you.
Psalm 32:8

For still the vision awaits its appointed time; it hastens to the end—it will not lie. If it seems slow, wait for it; it will surely come; it will not delay.
Habakkuk 2:3

And let us not grow weary of doing good, for in due season we will reap, if we do not give up.
Galatians 6:9

He put a new song in my mouth, a song of praise to our God. Many will see and fear, and put their trust in the Lord.
Psalm 40:3

Michael Gasaway

Dreams of You

As dawn approached the first rays of sunlight shot through the
heavens like flaming spears;
His voice from her dreams she could still hear ringing in her
ears.

The sunlight danced in her eyes like the setting sun on the
Caribbean Sea;
She searched the horizon for where her true love might be.

Her hair shimmered in the early morning dawn, reflecting the sun
in her hair like spun gold shining in the sunlight;
For her it had been another lonely night.

Her lips were crimson and moist with a whisper of hope, truth
and love;
She so wanted her prayer answered from above.

Her beauty was all this and so much more;
Like her outward beauty so was she within which shown through
the warmth of her smile that could warm you to your very core.

She held onto her heart's desire knowing someday he would
come to set her free to love again;
This is the hope she held and heard with the sound of the warm
southern wind.

They had not met as of yet, but from her dreams, of him she
knew;
He was the one man that would speak to her heart, and to her
always be true.

Then one day across the meadow she saw a cowboy come riding
up the trail;
In the distance she could hear the lonely sound of a wolf wail.

Almost instantly they touched with their eyes and held each
other with their hearts;
She knew then that from him, she would never want to be
apart.

He slowly walked toward her, tipped his hat and started to say....
When she reached up and kissed him. He pulled her
close and gazed deep into her green eyes and kissed her back
in a passionate but tender special way.

Their many trails are yet to be ridden and their story is just
beginning;
But together they now ride side by side looking forward to a
love never ending.

∿∿∿

For nothing will be impossible with God. Luke 1:37

*And let us not grow weary of doing good, for in due season we
will reap, if we do not give up.* Galatians 6:9

*For I know the plans I have for you, declares the Lord, plans for
welfare and not for evil, to give you a future and a hope.*
Jeremiah 29:11

*And we know that for those who love God all things work
together for good, for those who are called according to his
purpose.* Romans 8:28

*Rejoice always, pray without ceasing, give thanks in all
circumstances; for this is the will of God in Christ Jesus for you. 1*
Thessalonians 5:16-18

*Delight yourself in the Lord, and he will give you the desires of
your heart.* Psalm 37:4

For where your treasure is, there your heart will be also.
Matthew 6:21

Michael Gasaway

Desires of Your Heart

"She brakes for birds", her kids laugh at her and say;
She'd never hurt another, as that's not her way.

Kind and gentle is her spirit that lies deep within;
And you are very lucky indeed to call her your friend.

Her beauty on the outside is what you will first see;
Oh but the beauty on the inside, is even more exquisite and even
harder to believe.

Her sweetness and kindness will leave you not knowing what to
say;
And her smile will brighten, even the darkest of days.

In her life she has seen more than her fair share of heartache
and pain;
Smiling she thinks back, and knows that the sunshine will return
after the storms and rain.

So, on she goes each day doing the best that she can;
In her heart sometimes she remembers the love of that one
special man.

She's not really sure what tomorrow may bring her way;
But once upon a time, she knew real love, along "Life's Highway".

So now into the future she goes day after day;
In her heart she secretly still prays that one day, true love will
come again and take her away.

God will give you the desires of your heart, I read in the Bible
one day;
I know this to be true, so for you, this I will always pray.

~~~

32

Be delighted with the Lord.
Then He will give you all the desires of your heart.
Psalms 37:4

The heart of man plans his way, but the Lord establishes his
steps.
Proverbs 16:9

But seek first the kingdom of God and his righteousness, and all
these things will be added to you.
Matthew 6:33

Wait for the Lord; be strong, and let your heart take courage;
wait for the Lord!
Psalm 27:14

For God gave us a spirit not of fear but of power and love and
self-control.
2 Timothy 1:7

And let us not grow weary of doing good, for in due season we
will reap, if we do not give up. Galatians 6:9

Michael Gasaway

A Different Road

How her emerald green eyes would sparkle and glow;
When across the dance floor she and her partner would go.

So effortlessly she seems to spin and twirl;
How she loved to be in this musical world.

Moving to the rhythm of the steel guitar and country beat;
She seems to float across the floor with clouds beneath her feet.

This is the world where her heart truly belongs;
Back in her younger days, up on that stage she sang the songs.

Being on that stage singing really made her feel so alive;
It was like no other emotion she has ever felt inside.

Singing is her passion and stirs her soul deep within;
It has always been that way from the beginning, and will be to
the very end.

The sounds of that fiddle and of a steel guitar twang;
Not only was it her voice, but it was also her heart that sang.

Now she just dances to the country beat;
How she often wonders how different her life might be.

Oh how she loves to watch and listen to a live country band rage;
Back in time it takes her, when she was singing up on that stage.

She'd love to be up on that stage and be singing;
Thinking back now it saddens her and fills her with a longing.

Somewhere along the way she took a different road you see;
Now she often wonders how different her life might be.

Leaving Nashville and her dreams behind, she took a different
road;
Now it fills her with sadness at times, as to how her life did
unfold.

Watching now from the floor instead of on the stage above;
It was music all along that was her one true love.

Music and singing could only touch her in that special way;
Oh how she misses and longs to be back up on that stage.

Settling now to be just part of the audience on the floor;
Remembering back to the applause and how the crowd did roar.

Now she's right there with them if there's a live country music to be heard;
Along with the band she'll sing each song, word for word.

Sometimes in life we take a different road it's true;
We never know where that road may lead or if it'll make us happy or blue.

Always pray to God above that He will guide your steps each day;
Keep trusting and believing that He will show you the way.

Never give up on your dreams and look back someday in regret;
Go forward each day, doing the best you can until you reach your last sunset.

~~~

Many are the plans in the mind of a man, but it is the purpose of the Lord that will stand. Proverbs 19:21

I can do all things through him who strengthens me. Philippians 4:13

I will instruct you and teach you in the way you should go; I will counsel you with my eye upon you. Psalm 32:8

For nothing will be impossible with God. Luke 1:37

Michael Gasaway

Back to Texas

Down to Texas as a young girl she came;
She was looking for fortune and fame.

Out to Happy's in Brackettville she came to rest;
There she put her talent and singing voice to the test.

Up on that stage, how she loved to sing;
It made her feel alive, like no other thing.

Then she decided to leave her hopes and dreams behind;
Back up north she traveled trying to ease her troubled mind.

The years went by and a family she raised;
Sometimes she dreamed of Texas as across the prairie she
gazed.

One day she heard and felt the call deep within her soul;
In her heart she knew, that back down to Texas she must go.

Off she went with her six string in the back;
With a pocket full of dreams south bound in her ole Cadillac.

South bound to that ole Fort Worth town;
She was looking to fulfill her dreams and no longer to wear a
frown.

In her heart, Texas is where she truly longed to be;
Now at last her heart was once again going to be set free.

Sundance square, the ole stockyards and of course, Billy Bob's;
Just seeing it all again just made her heart throb.

Now at last back to Texas she had come;
To play that red dirt music, sing her songs no longer feeling
numb.

Up on that stage now you can find her most any night;
Playing her guitar and singing her songs with such delight.

Yes she followed her dream and never gave up;
Now back in Texas to stay, living life at a full gallop.

~~~

I can do all things through him who strengthens me.
Philippians 4:13

For nothing will be impossible with God. Luke 1:37

And let us not grow weary of doing good, for in due season we will reap, if we do not give up. Galatians 6:9

For I know the plans I have for you, declares the Lord, plans for welfare and not for evil, to give you a future and a hope.
Jeremiah 29:11

And we know that for those who love God all things work together for good, for those who are called according to his purpose. Romans 8:28

But you, take courage! Do not let your hands be weak, for your work shall be rewarded. 2 Chronicles 15:7

And without faith it is impossible to please him, for whoever would draw near to God must believe that he exists and that he rewards those who seek him. Hebrews 11:6

Fear not, for I am with you; be not dismayed, for I am your God; I will strengthen you, I will help you, I will uphold you with my righteous right hand. Isaiah 41:10

Michael Gasaway

TEXAS

If you have never been there it is so very hard to explain;
But one thing is sure, that once you go there, you'll never be the
same.

The people there are so different, and treat you just like a friend;
You'll soon realize that on them, you can depend.

There are plenty of wide open spaces for you to see;
The vistas you behold will make it so hard to believe.

Rolling hills, sunny beaches or endless plains;
And yes, even a desert that never sees much rain.

It's so full of history and helped to make our country great;
Once it was a republic before it became a state.

Cattle, cotton and horses just seem to be all around;
Yes, even black gold can still be found.

Indian blankets and bluebonnets cover the hill sides in the
spring;
The sight will stir your soul, with such a sweet longing.

It is mentioned in country music more than any other place;
It just seems to be filled with, God's amazing grace.

They have their own brand of music to them the best yet;
They even have their very own dance; they call the Texas Two
Step.

Some cowboys and cowgirls still call this place home;
And you can be sure that far from it, they will never want to
roam.

After sunset and it does become night;
You can look up toward heaven and see the stars so big and
bright.

Its flag flies next to the stars and stripes side by side;

It alone has this privilege and fills its people with much
pride.

It's as long as it is wide;
And will take you a day or more just to travel it from side to
side.

The pride of its people they carry within;
Can be seen on their faces when they say, "howdy" and smile
that big ole TEXAS grin.

Their BBQ is different from all the rest, and is the greatest all
around;
Not even Memphis or KC can compete, when they come to
town.

They take their sports to an extreme;
On Friday nights down there, football is more than just a
game.

The sky is so blue and stretches across the horizon for you to
see;
And yes they even have their own, deep blue sea.

The women there have no equal across this great land;
They can hold their very own, even with a man.

They have a special beauty that comes from deep within;
It's enough to make a man, want to go back again.

You'll find no place quite like it and I for one can't wait to go
back;
That's where you'll find me, just as soon as I pack.

The Great Lone Star State of TEXAS is the best this side of
those golden streets above;
Yes I'm going back to the promise land, back to the place I
dearly love.

~~~

By faith he went to live in the land of promise...... Hebrews 11:9

Michael Gasaway

The Round Pen

Have you ever found yourself in the round pen of life?
Sometimes it's where God puts us, so He can teach us to handle
strife.

Round pens can be a very useful tool in training a horse;
It's also how God uses things in life to keep us on His proper
course.

We use a round pen for teaching horses the way to go;
God does the same thing in life, when His will for us He tries to
show.

A round pen can be used to teach horses to overcome obstacles
on the trail;
So it is with God when He sees us starting to fail.

The round pen helps teach a horse good forward movement;
With us, God does the same thing when He tries to get us in
alignment.

In the round pen you want the horse thinking about just you, and
not looking all about;
As it is with God as He prepares you for your new life breakout.

Horses in the round pen you teach that he has to give its control
over to you;
That is the same thing that God is trying to do.

Next time you find yourself in life's round pen;
Remember that now, is the time to let go and give it all to Him.

~~~

Be anxious for nothing, but in everything by prayer and supplication, with thanksgiving, let your requests be made known to God.
Philippians 4:6

For I know the plans I have for you, declares the Lord, plans for welfare and not for evil, to give you a future and a hope.
Jeremiah 29:11

And we know that for those who love God all things work together for good, for those who are called according to his purpose.
Romans 8:28

Count it all joy, my brothers, when you meet trials of various kinds, for you know that the testing of your faith produces steadfastness. And let steadfastness have its full effect, that you may be perfect and complete, lacking in nothing.
James 1:2-4

Take my yoke upon you, and learn from me, for I am gentle and lowly in heart, and you will find rest for your souls.
Matthew 11:29

I can do all things through him who strengthens me.
Philippians 4:13

Restoration

A cowboy sat on a bench in the stockyards of ole' Fort Worth
town;
Wearing his Stetson hat, favorite boots and a checkered button
down.

Not many of the tourists seemed to notice him as they walked
by;
Occasionally one would nod their head at him or just say hi.

Little did they know, that he was a cowboy poet of some renown;
There he sat thinking back with a smile, no longer wearing that
frown.

This cowboy was like a modern day David from biblical times;
He was speaking to and about God, through his words and
rhymes.

His own giants he has also faced and slain during his life;
He'd even experienced the same losses as David along with other
strife.

Of love, fear, hope and faith he wrote of in his many rhymes;
Never did he lose his own faith, even during the darkest of times.

Tried he did to find joy in all situations and kept trusting in God
above;
No matter the circumstances he would trust in God's mercy and
love.

One day he knew that God again would show him mercy and
grace;
And that God would restore all that had been lost during his life's
race.

Then one day just as he believed it would, it all started to come
to pass;
Restoration began, of all that had been lost, God even
surpassed.

Never give up and keep your faith and trust in God above;
Then one day your dreams will be fulfilled with God's mercy
and love.

It's up to you to believe that your best God does have in store;
Keep praying and knocking, then one day, God will open that door.

The door to your heart's desire and all the prayers that you said;
He will in His time answer all of your prayers, they may be just ahead.

So be thankful and joyful in all the things, that do come each day;
Adversity and happy times are both preparing you and showing you the way.

As it was for David as the Bible said, so it will be for you to see;
Restoration of all lost, plus dreams fulfilled, when you awaken to your new destiny.

∼∼∼

Delight thyself also in the LORD: and he shall give thee the desires of thine heart. Commit thy way unto the LORD; trust also in him; and he shall bring it to pass. Psalm 37:4-5

Turn you to the stronghold, ye prisoners of hope: even to-day do I declare that I will render double unto thee.
Zechariah 9:12

Keep Asking, Seeking, Knocking
"So I say to you, ask, and it will be given to you; seek, and you will find; knock, and it will be opened to you. For everyone who asks receives, and he who seeks finds, and to him who knocks it will be opened. Luke 11:9-10

Michael Gasaway

Men of Velvet and Steel

Her heart had been wounded by love's failures once more;
She wondered if true love would ever again knock at her door.

All seemed to know how to talk the talk and make her laugh and smile;
But it only seemed to last for a very short while.

Where have all the real men gone she wondered in her mind?
A real man who not only knew right from wrong, but could also be gentle and kind.

What has happened to those men who had both a strong and gentle will?
Those who were once called, men of velvet and steel.

The men of old, who could be tough as leather and hard as steel;
But they knew how and when to be even softer still.

You could depend on them, and have no doubt about what they sought;
They were the men you could trust, who also walked the walk.

Still they exist out there but are fewer now it seems;
Just keep looking and one day you'll find the man of your dreams.

You don't have to settle, worry or rush you see;
Leave it up to God, trust in Him, and just believe.

~~~

May he give you the desire of your heart and make all your plans succeed. May we shout for joy over your victory and lift up our banners in the name of our God. May the LORD grant all your requests?
Psalm 20:4-5

Trust in the Lord with all your heart, and do not lean on your own understanding. In all your ways acknowledge him, and he will make straight your paths.
Proverbs 3:5-6

For nothing will be impossible with God.
Luke 1:37

The glory of young men is their strength, but the splendor of old men is their gray hair.
Proverbs 20:29

A faithful man will abound with blessings..
Proverbs 28:20

Whatever you do, work heartily, as for the Lord and not for men,
Colossians 3:23

For we are his workmanship, created in Christ Jesus for   good works, which God prepared beforehand, that we should walk in them. Ephesians 2:10

He who walks blamelessly and does what is right and speaks truth in his heart;
Psalm 15:2

Michael Gasaway

Life's Not Fair

The cotton candy clouds drifted across the Texas sky;
As a single tear fell from her dazzling blue eyes.

Like the clouds above, her thoughts drifted back in time;
She thought of him, her feelings so sublime.

Once upon a time, she felt the rush of love;
It had come upon her, as if from lightning above.

Still she remembers his gentle touch and penetrating gaze;
Now in her mind, that memory replays.

In the distance she hears the river rushing by;
She remembers back to that special night beneath a star filled
sky.

Oh how she can still feel his passionate kisses upon her skin;
Never had she felt such feelings from deep within.

Sometimes we make the choices as we travel life's road;
Other times choices are made for us, by what we are told.

Life's not fair; I've heard it said many times over the years;
The lessons we learn, often come with painful tears.

It's all about the lessons learned, and the choices we make;
There are times you don't get to choose which road you take.

Now alone she travels, down this lonesome road of life;
Wondering why her life was filled with so much strife.

Then a smile slowly crosses her beautiful face;
Realizing that it's not how you start, but how you finish life's
race.

So into tomorrow she walks with a purposeful stride;
Yes, it's time to Cowgirl Up, and give it one more try.

~~~

I can do all things through him who strengthens me.
Philippians 4:13

And let us not grow weary of doing good, for in due season we
will reap, if we do not give up. *Galatians 6:9*

For I know the plans I have for you, declares the Lord, plans for
welfare and not for evil, to give you a future and a hope.
Jeremiah 29:11

And we know that for those who love God all things work
together for good, for those who are called according to his
purpose. *Romans 8:28*

Rejoice always, pray without ceasing, give thanks in all
circumstances; for this is the will of God in Christ Jesus for you. *1*
Thessalonians 5:16-18

Delight yourself in the Lord, and he will give you the desires of
your heart. *Psalm 37:4*

So then let us pursue what makes for peace and for mutual up
building. *Romans 14:19*

He will wipe away every tear from their eyes, and death
shall be no more, neither shall there be mourning, nor crying, nor
pain anymore, for the former things have passed away."
Revelation 21:4

Michael Gasaway

On an Autumn Breeze

She came to him on an autumn breeze and set him free;
Then she showed him true love, and all that it could be.

It was a romance that was born in an unusual way to be sure;
But this love they shared together was oh so pure.

Both had faced losses and heartache in the past;
Each looked at the other knowing that this love would last.

Neither was looking when God led them to each other on that fall
day;
But their hearts were open, so that God could lead the way.

You never know when love will come calling at your door;
Just keep your heart receptive for the one you will always adore.

Their life together is just beginning as I write their story in
rhyme;
This is a true love that will indeed stand the test of time.

Pray for them and all that seek to find true love along the way;
Never give up on love and a true unconditional love will find you
one day.

~~~

And above all these put on love, which binds everything together in perfect harmony.
Colossians 3:14

With all humility and gentleness, with patience, bearing with one another in love,
Ephesians 4:2

Love is patient and kind; love does not envy or boast; it is   not arrogant or rude. It does not insist on its own way; it is not irritable or resentful; it does not rejoice at wrongdoing, but rejoices with the truth. Love bears all things, believes all things, hopes all things, endures all things.
1 Corinthians 13:4-7

And let us not grow weary of doing good, for in due season we will reap, if we do not give up. Galatians 6:9

For I know the plans I have for you, declares the Lord, plans for welfare and not for evil, to give you a future and a hope.
Jeremiah 29:11

Michael Gasaway

A Smile Crosses Her Face

Wanting to again to let herself feel and have love awaken;
To know that special feeling that seems to warm her like the sun.

How her body aches to be held and feel the touch of that one
special man.
Sometimes she wonders if she has let love slip by, like an hour
glass of sand.

Remembering his eyes, how they seemed to penetrate into her
very soul.
The warmth of his touch could keep her warm against the cold.

She recalls just how the sound of his voice would turn her on;
His voice and words seem to come from some ole love song.

Fondly she recalls that first kiss, and what she felt deep inside.
He made something start stirring, she once again was feeling
alive.

Yes, she remembers how she once came close, but fear had
stopped her cold.
Her heart tried to push her on, but her head said no.

Now down Life's Highway she travels, some days feeling more
like leather than lace.
Then she remembers that sweet cowboy, and a smile crosses her
face.

~~~

And above all these put on love, which binds everything together in perfect harmony.
Colossians 3:14

For God gave us a spirit not of fear but of power and love and self-control.
2 Timothy 1:7

There is no fear in love, but perfect love casts out fear. For fear has to do with punishment, and whoever fears has not been perfected in love.
1 John 4:18

Have I not commanded you? Be strong and courageous. Do not be frightened, and do not be dismayed, for the Lord your God is with you wherever you go.
Joshua 1:9

And we know that for those who love God all things work together for good, for those who are called according to his purpose. Romans 8:28

Peace I leave with you; my peace I give to you. Not as the world gives do I give to you. Let not your hearts be troubled, neither let them be afraid. John 14:27

Michael Gasaway

Dreams Come True

Alone and empty she had felt most of her life;
All she knew was heartache, pain, suffering and strife.

Her faith in God was the only refuge she had known at times;
Giving up was never an option nor did it ever cross her mind.

A long and hard road it had been, for her and her little buckaroo;
Sometimes she wondered if her dreams would ever come true.

Then one day she was struck by the words that she read;
And she realized then, that her dreams were not really dead.

Now she realized that her destiny was hers to claim;
It was now time to Cowgirl Up, and no longer cast any blame.

Resurrecting dreams she had once held so dear;
Into the future she goes now, with a plan that she see's so clear.

One by one into action her plans started to fall into place;
In her heart she knows that it's due to God's amazing grace.

God places your dreams and destiny in your own two hands;
It's up to you and Him and not as the world demands.

Put your hands together and pray, listen to what God has to
say;
Then use your hands to do the work as he directs you each day.

He placed those dreams within each person's heart;
They have been with you from the beginning, waiting for you to
start.

So start today without delay and do what God is directing you to
do;
Remember it's never too late to make all your dreams come
true.

You never really know what you can do until you try;
Keep pushing forward and never let your dreams die.

You'll look back one day and realize your dreams have all
come true;

And realize you were never alone, as God was always with you.

God Bless all you dreamers of dreams out there, far and wide;
Never Give Up, keep trusting in God and cast all your doubts and fears aside.

~~~

And we know that for those who love God all things work together for good, for those who are called according to his purpose. Romans 8:28

For I know the plans I have for you, declares the Lord, plans for welfare and not for evil, to give you a future and a hope. Then you will call upon me and come and pray to me, and I will hear you. You will seek me and find me, when you seek me with all your heart. Jeremiah 29:11-13

For nothing will be impossible with God. Luke 1:37

Delight yourself in the Lord, and he will give you the desires of your heart. Psalm 37:4

I can do all things through him who strengthens me. Philippians 4:13

And let us not grow weary of doing good, for in due season we will reap, if we do not give up. Galatians 6:9

Michael Gasaway

Circuit Rider

Saddlebag preacher, circuit rider and other names he's heard;
Riding the dusty trails, he preaches God's word.

From town to town across this land he does ride;
It's just him and God, riding side by side.

Preaching the word and an occasional wedding he does perform;
Black hat, white shirt and duster are his uniform.

His Bible is dusty and torn here and there;
But when he preaches God's word, there is fire in the air.

Many a soul he has saved along the way;
He's taught farmer and cowboy alike, how to pray.

Across this vast land he rode from shore to shore;
The circuit rider has been God's faithful ambassador.

To believers and non he did God's word impart;
Along the way being a blessing to many a pioneer's heart.

His saddle is his pulpit and his church the wide open sky;
He's a saddlebag hero, preaching God's word far and wide.

Gone but not forgotten are these stout men of old;
They braved countless dangers so God's word could be told.

Many a church today can trace their roots to one of these brave
men;
The saddlebag preachers, who tried to save man from sin.

~~~

And he said to them, "Go into all the world and proclaim the gospel to the whole creation".
Mark 16:15

Preach the word; be ready in season and out of season; reprove, rebuke, and exhort, with complete patience and teaching.
2 Timothy 4:2

Do your best to present yourself to God as one approved, a worker who has no need to be ashamed, rightly handling the word of truth.
2 Timothy 2:15

Not many of you should become teachers, my brothers, for you know that we who teach will be judged with greater strictness.
James 3:1

All Scripture is breathed out by God and profitable for teaching, for reproof, for correction, and for training in righteousness,
2 Timothy 3:16

Go therefore and make disciples of all nations, baptizing them in the name of the Father and of the Son and of the Holy Spirit,
Matthew 28:19

And we impart this in words not taught by human wisdom but taught by the Spirit, interpreting spiritual truths to those who are spiritual.
1 Corinthians 2:13

Michael Gasaway

A Mother's Prayers

You raise your children and try to do the best that you know;
Then one day they grow up and it's time to let them go.

It's never an easy process as you were there every step of their way;
After all, you're the reason they even have a birthday.

Over the years you did your best to raise them right;
And you still continue to pray for them, each and every night.

Sometimes they did things that brought you such joy and happiness;
A special card, I love you or just a hug and gentle kiss.

There were times that they could make you so mad;
At night you would cry yourself to sleep, and feel so sad.

Overnight they seem to grow up and then one day they move away;
Sometimes that can be the hardest time, and for them, you continue to pray.

As they become adults, sometimes it's even harder on you than before;
They seem to know it all and don't seem to need you as often anymore.

Now the heartache and pain can be worse than when they were a child;
But keep praying for them and their loving ways will return in awhile.

Mother's prayers seem to have a special meaning to God up above;
I guess that's because like with Him, they come with unconditional love.

The joy and happiness will always outweigh the sadness and pain in the end;
You just need to love them through it, and let them know on you, they can depend.

So pray for them every night and trust God that the right thing
they will always try to do;
Then one day they will return with a hug, a kiss and say;
thank you Mom, I Love You.

∾∾∾

*But they who wait for the Lord shall renew their strength; they
shall mount up with wings like eagles; they shall run and not be
weary; they shall walk and not faint.*
Isaiah 40:31

We love because he first loved us.
1 John 4:19

*Her children rise up and call her blessed; her husband also, and
he praises her:*
Proverbs 31:28

*For I know the plans I have for you, declares the Lord, plans for
welfare and not for evil, to give you a future and a hope.*
Jeremiah 29:11

Michael Gasaway

The Note

Things seemed to be more hectic ever since she found herself
alone;
She does her best, to still make her house a home.

Never did she ever imagine that her life would turn out this way;
Now she just does her best to make it through each day.

Making breakfast and lunches for her kids each morning;
They are her priority now and taking care of them keeps her
going.

Some days she doesn't know how she will handle all the stress;
It's late at night that she feels the pain of her loneliness.

Getting her kids off to school and herself off to her job;
This is her life now and at times makes her sob.

Into her pocket she reaches for the keys to her car;
Out came a note from her son that left her ajar.

"Thank you for all you do for sis and I", the note in part read;
"We love you Mom…..just because" at the end is what it said.

Raising kids alone is no easy task be it woman or man;
Just know that you're appreciated and your children are your
biggest fan.

Not always showing it each day by what they do and say;
But know that they are heeding all the words and actions you
display.

Just do your best and let God show you the way;
Let your children see God through you, by what you say and do
each day.

God give strength to all you single Moms and Dads out there
doing your best;
May God always guide your steps and know that you will be
blessed.

~~~

Train up a child in the way he should go; even when he is old he will not depart from it.
Proverbs 22:6

Do not be anxious about anything, but in everything by prayer and supplication with thanksgiving let your requests be made known to God. And the peace of God, which surpasses all understanding, will guard your hearts and your minds in Christ Jesus.
Philippians 4:6,7

Casting all your anxieties on him, because he cares for you.
1 Peter 5:7

I can do all things through him who strengthens me.
Philippians 4:13

Be strong and courageous. Do not fear or be in dread of them, for it is the Lord your God who goes with you. He will not leave you or forsake you.
Deuteronomy 31:6

For the Lord your God is he who goes with you to fight for you against your enemies, to give you the victory.
Deuteronomy 20:4

Michael Gasaway

True Destiny

The loss of love comes with its own special pain;
Some days your tears will flow like a spring rain.

Their choice, your choice or God's up above;
The pain is all the same if you were in love.

Real or imaginary, the pain is all the same;
It will leave you feeling as if you're going insane.

You struggle to get through each day with all your might;
Then the veil of loneliness comes with the darkness of night.

You try to forget and push them far from your mind;
But somehow they just seem to creep in again time after time.

Only time will loosen the grip of the pain you now feel;
As hard as you try, the day and nights become so surreal.

One day you will awaken with the rising of the sun;
You then realize that your new life has just begun.

So live each day the best you can, regret free;
It's up to you now, to passionately pursue your true destiny.

~~~

For I know the plans I have for you, declares the Lord, plans for welfare and not for evil, to give you a future and a hope. Jeremiah 29:11

More than that, we rejoice in our sufferings, knowing that suffering produces endurance, and endurance produces character, and character produces hope, and hope does not put us to shame, because God's love has been poured into our hearts through the Holy Spirit who has been given to us. Romans 5:3-5

For still the vision awaits its appointed time; it hastens to the end—it will not lie. If it seems slow, wait for it; it will surely come; it will not delay. Habakkuk 2:3

The Lord will fulfill his purpose for me; your steadfast love, O Lord, endures forever. Do not forsake the work of your hands. Psalm 138:8

Therefore I tell you, whatever you ask in prayer, believe that you have received it, and it will be yours. Mark 11:24

Michael Gasaway

Regrets

She sat atop the mountain and watched the sun slowly set;
Into the fading rays of light, she saw her every last regret.

Climbing up to the top she had come to find peace;
Now she realized that what she really needed was release.

Release of the past and any regrets she still carried within;
It was time to stop blaming herself and to begin again.

The lies you tell and the mistakes you made;
Without amends, they'll come to haunt you on a distant day.

God may lead you back to the past to make amends;
Or tell you to leave it all behind you, along with all your sins.

You can't move forward to receive what God has planned;
If you're still reaching back into the past with one hand.

Let go and let God have complete control of your life;
Give it all to him, especially all of life's strife.

Then reach out with both hands to receive what He wants to
give;
Start the day out fresh, and once again really begin to live.

There is a new day that will be coming with the sun,
It's time to start living again and to start having some fun.

Now it's up to you to decide if you're going to win or lose;
God has given you the free will to choose.

With the dawning and as each new day does begin;
Whatever in life you choose to do, always be in it to win.

Pray for God's forgiveness and guidance in everything you do;
Keep praying and believing as He is always with you.

Now go live your life to the fullest, the best that you can;
Walk into tomorrow with your head held high, following God's
plan.

~~~

But one thing I do: forgetting what lies behind and straining forward to what lies ahead, I press on toward the goal for the prize of the upward call of God in Christ Jesus. Let those of us who are mature think this way, and if in anything you think otherwise, God will reveal that also to you.
Philippians 3:13-15

If we confess our sins, he is faithful and just to forgive us our sins and to cleanse us from all unrighteousness.
1 John 1:9

Be kind to one another, tenderhearted, forgiving one another, as God in Christ forgave you.
Ephesians 4:32

For I know the plans I have for you, declares the Lord, plans for welfare and not for evil, to give you a future and a hope.
Jeremiah 29:11

"The Lord will fight for you, and you have only to be silent."
Exodus 14:14

The heart of man plans his way, but the Lord establishes his steps. Proverbs 16:9

Michael Gasaway

The Great Potter's Hands

We never truly know what tomorrow may bring;
Will it be heartache and pain, or maybe a new love song to sing?

Each new day is a fresh page we get to write our story upon;
Some days we write of love and hope, some days, how we can't
go on.

Sometimes we may not understand what God for us has planned;
But always remember we are but clay in the great potter's hands.

Using our trials to reshape us in His, own way;
We may not understand it all, at least not today.

Molding you and shaping you into that which you need to
become;
Purifying and strengthening you as He adds additional wisdom.

It's not our job to understand His mysterious ways up on high;
We just need to believe He's in control and to not always ask,
"Why God why?"

So when you face that time in life and know not which way to go;
Just remember that God is with you and the right way He will
show.

Always with you he will be every step that you take along the
way;
Not just with you is He, when you take time to pray.

Never lose sight of whose child you really are;
He's the one that created you, along with each and every star.

So put a smile on your face and a song in your heart to sing;
For with each new day, comes the promise of God's new
blessing.

~~~

Yet you, LORD, are our Father. We are the clay, you are the potter; we are all the work of your hand.
Isaiah 64:8

For I know the plans I have for you, declares the Lord, plans for welfare and not for evil, to give you a future and a hope.
Jeremiah 29:11

For we are his workmanship, created in Christ Jesus for good works, which God prepared beforehand, that we should walk in them.
Ephesians 2:10

Before I formed you in the womb I knew you, and before you were born I consecrated you; I appointed you a prophet to the nations.
Jeremiah 1:5

And we know that for those who love God all things work together for good, for those who are called according to his purpose.
Romans 8:28

Michael Gasaway

Vessel of Clay

Slowly she began to feel empty inside with each passing day;
Drying out within was she and beginning to crack, just like a
jar of clay.

Each day she poured out more and more, all that she had;
Until one day, all she really felt inside was very, very sad.

She always had a kind word and something nice to say;
It was at home feeling the stress of the day that the clay was
beginning to give way.

Day by day she was pouring out more than she took in;
On the outside she was smiling but feeling more broken
within.

Just like a fine vessel made of clay;
God has formed each one of us, all in much the same way.

Clay vessels were made to hold wine, water and many things;
They must be replenished, just as does the rains of spring.

People are no different it seems to me;
When you are constantly giving and pouring out, then empty
you'll soon be.

You must be refilled from time to time with words of life;
Otherwise you will begin to feel and see only strife.

Try to fill each person you know with a kind word each day;
Sometimes just a simple text or written note is the best way.

For if not, like a clay vessel, cracked and broken in time they
will become;
If they are left empty and only feeling lost and numb.

Never do you know what trials in life they have seen or
been through;
So give them a kind word or even say; I love you.

Ones that appear the strongest on the outside suffer in
silence until it's too late;
Don't let that be yours or a friend's fate.

The seemingly strongest you know may need some praise
and kind words the most;
They are the ones always giving and never boast.

Reach out today to someone you know and pour out living
words of praise;
Don't let someone you know become a cracked vessel of
clay.

Next time a friend or stranger you meet along the way;
A smile and hello, a well done, you're awesome or a word of
praise is the least you can say.

Always remember that even the strongest person you may
meet along life's highway;
Are still but a mere vessel and have feet made of clay.

∿∿∿

*Pleasant words [are as] an honeycomb, sweet to the soul, and
health to the bones.*
Proverbs 16:24

*A soft answer turns away wrath, but a harsh word stirs up
anger.* Proverbs 15:1

*Let no corrupting talk come out of your mouths, but only such
as is good for building up, as fits the occasion, that it may give
grace to those who hear.*
Ephesians 4:29

*Therefore encourage one another and build one another up,
just as you are doing.*
1 Thessalonians 5:11

Michael Gasaway

Mountains and Faith

The Bible says that with faith you can move mountains if you just
believe;
All it takes it says, is but the faith of a tiny mustard seed.

I've seen God's miracles happen in my life, time and again;
But when faced with a new mountain, sometimes you forget just
how to win.

So just trust God up above and keep working at it daily and
never ever give up;
As God will always provide all that you need, along with His
merciful love.

It also says in that just having faith without works is dead;
You must work hard, do your best, and always keep looking to
the prize up ahead.

The prize you seek is that which lies beyond the mountain that
you now see;
Maybe it's your one true love, an answered prayer, or your life's
destiny.

Don't slacken your pace or take your eyes off that which you now
seek;
You must give it your all and work through it, now's not the time
to be weak.

Face every mountain that comes your way with faith, courage
and peace;
Sometimes when you feel that you can't go on, that's when the
prize is just within your reach.

Thank God for every mountain along life's road that you have to
face;
And remember it's not how you start that matters, but how you
finish life's race.

Remember the lessons well so that you can help another
when to you they turn;
For with each new mountain a new life lesson you will learn.

So the next time a mountain does block your way, put a smile
on your face;
Just believe that something wonderful is on the other side,
and you will succeed with faith and God's amazing grace.

∿∿∿

*I tell you the truth, if anyone says to this mountain, 'Go, throw
yourself into the sea, 'and does not doubt in his heart but
believes that what he says will happen, it will be done for him.*
Mark 11:2

*....For if you had the faith even as small as a tiny   mustard
seed you could say to this mountain, 'Move!' and it would go far
away. Nothing would be impossible.*
Matthew 17:20

*Now faith is the assurance of things hoped for, the conviction of
things not seen.*
Hebrews 11:1

*And whatever you ask in prayer, you will receive, if you have
faith.*
Matthew 21:22

I can do all things through him who strengthens me.
Philippians 4:13

Life's Storms

They all occupy space and time somewhere deep in your mind;
You get to decide which you will give the space and time.

The ones that you spend time with and feed the most will grow
and grow;
It's up to you and your thoughts as to which ones will take
control.

Choose whether you will rise high and soar like an eagle and win;
Or will you let worry and fear drive you down into a fatal tailspin.

When you face that storm in life and you're being thrown all
about;
Waves are crashing in upon you, and you just want to shout.

Will you choose Faith and Hope or Worry and Fear?
The one you pick could have an everlasting affect on the rest of
your year.

Don't wait until the storm clouds start to gather in your life;
Decide today how and what you will do in those times of strife.

Read His word and take time out each day to pray;
Ask God to prepare your heart by taking all the fear and worry
away.

It won't be easy to do as most of us have been feeding fear for
years;
So put the time and energy in now or later cry the tears.

Your life will be so much happier and filled with joy and
peace;
When you let go of worry and fear, give it to God and just
release.

God Bless all that struggle with the demons of fear and worry
each day;
I hope that you will learn to find joy and peace, even in life's
storms I pray.

~~~

For God did not give us a spirit of fear, but of power and of love and of self-control.
2 Timothy 1:7

When the tempest passes, the wicked is no more, but the righteous is established forever.
Proverbs 10:25

Do not be anxious about anything, but in everything by prayer and supplication with thanksgiving let your requests be made known to God. And the peace of God, which surpasses all understanding, will guard your hearts and your minds in Christ Jesus.
Philippians 4:6-7

Peace I leave with you; my peace I give to you. Not as the world gives do I give to you. Let not your hearts be troubled, neither let them be afraid.
John 14:27

Michael Gasaway

As Time Goes By

Letting go is never an easy thing to do whether it be in life or
death;
Sometimes it's how we grow and learn the importance of each
breath.

It comes with such a pain that you think will never go away;
Try as we might the pain seems to grow stronger each day.

As time goes by, the pain will lessen its grip on your heart;
Then the sun will shine again as you begin your new life's walk.

So don't give up or think of giving in;
As you could be just a moment away, from God's new blessin'.

Put a smile on your face and a song in our heart;
For this is a new day, and for you, a fresh new start.

Walk forward into tomorrow as the best of your life is yet to be;
Open your eyes and see clearly that which waits, is your new
destiny.

Expect the best this new life has to offer;
Then go boldly forward, in time the meaning you will discover.

Leave the past behind you, but remember the lessons well;
Then someday when it's your time, your story you can tell.

~~~

Trust in the Lord with all your heart, and do not lean on your own understanding. In all your ways acknowledge him, and he will make straight your paths.
Proverbs 3:5-6

For I know the plans I have for you, declares the Lord, plans for welfare and not for evil, to give you a future and a hope.
Jeremiah 29:11

"Remember not the former things, nor consider the things of old. Behold, I am doing a new thing; now it springs forth, do you not perceive it? I will make a way in the wilderness and rivers in the desert."
Isaiah 43:18-19

Do not be anxious about anything, but in everything by prayer and supplication with thanksgiving let your requests be made known to God.
Philippians 4:6

Michael Gasaway

Addicted

It started out so innocent as most addictions do, just a few pills
each day;
Slowly the amount needed increased just so she could find a
way.

She told herself she was not addicted and it was just for the
pain;
But with lies and deceitfulness, there never is any gain.

Treatment center one after another she found herself within;
Then clean for a few months or a year, and then she was back
again.

She attended the meetings and sometimes felt she could win;
The chips added up, but in the end once again she gave in.

Never realizing the damage to her marriage and family she did;
Her husband stood beside her and from her sons kept the secret
hid.

The boys knew something was wrong but thought it may have
been them;
So instead of being a mother, she tried to be more like a friend.

Too much for her to bear as she realized what she had done;
Now selfishly she leaves behind a grieving husband and her sons.

Never too late to really change and make a new life;
Don't let giving up be your legacy causing your family endless
strife.

As you see, addicts never really see the damage that they do;
Sometimes becoming a generational curse that they put
future generations through.

Some people are addicted to love quite literally so;
Then others take drugs or alcohol and can't seem to let go.

Addiction is all the same no matter what you're addicted
too;
You must seek help before it's too late and pray God leads
you through.

Won't be easy and will be the hardest challenge you ever
face;
Just keep trusting in God and His amazing grace.

One day your future will be bright as the noon day sun;
That's when you will realize that at least one battle is won.

The war will never be over for you, as each day on you must
fight;
But the hardest is behind you now and you're no longer
afraid of the night.

Just keep trusting and believing and ask God for the strength
to get by;
This is your new life now and seeking forgiveness is
something you should try.

Forgive yourself and then those that you may have hurt
along the way;
Don't forget to thank the ones that stood by you through
endless nights and longer days.

Never give up and start fresh with each new day;
Make up for those lost years and help another along
"Life's Highway".

~~~

I can do all things through him who strengthens me.
Philippians 4:13

*For God did not give us a spirit of fear, but of power and of love
and of self-control.*
2 Timothy 1:7

"The Lord will fight for you, and you have only to be silent."
Exodus 14:14

Michael Gasaway

Survivor

Into the doctor's office they came to wait for the news;
She just stared silently at her brand new shoes.

Quiet was the office as alone they sat together;
They tightly held hands, knowing this storm they would weather.

The doctor's expression said it all, as he came through the door;
In an instant they knew, as their hearts hit the floor.

Calmly the doctor explained his plan;
They now knew, it was all in God's hands.

Surgery will be the first step that we must take;
We need to act fast, for your sake.

There will be rounds of radiation and chemo you'll have to bear;
But all she could do was just sit there and stare.

Chances are real good, as I think we found it in time,
This news somewhat eased her troubled mind.

Days, weeks and months slowly drug by;
Sometimes she found herself asking; "why God why?"

It's only natural to wonder at a time like this and ask God why;
Just remember to never give up and on you must try.

Some days will be good and some will be bad;
Keep a smile in your heart and try not to be sad.

Struggle on each day the best that you can;
Know that God holds you in the palm of his hand.

Pray for strength and courage from God above;
And in time you'll feel his unconditional love.

Then one day a bright future you will see;
That's when you hear your doctor say; "You're cancer free".

So put your hands together with me and let's all say a prayer,
For all those who battle against cancer, everyday and
everywhere.

∾∾∾

Heal me, O Lord, and I shall be healed; save me, and I shall be saved, for you are my praise.
Jeremiah 17:14

Fear not, for I am with you; be not dismayed, for I am your God; I will strengthen you, I will help you, I will uphold you with my righteous right hand.
Isaiah 41:10

Bless the Lord, O my soul, and forget not all his benefits, who forgives all your iniquity, who heals all your diseases, who redeems your life from the pit, who crowns you with steadfast love and mercy,
Psalm 103:2-4

And the prayer of faith will save the one who is sick, and the Lord will raise him up. And if he has committed sins, he will be forgiven. James 5:15

Is anyone among you sick? Let him call for the elders of the church, and let them pray over him, anointing him with oil in the name of the Lord. And the prayer of faith will save the one who is sick, and the Lord will raise him up. And if he has committed sins, he will be forgiven. Therefore, confess your sins to one another and pray for one another, that you may be healed. The prayer of a righteous person has great power as it is working.
James 5:14-16

The Lord sustains him on his sickbed; in his illness you restore him to full health.
Psalm 41:3

Michael Gasaway

When it's Time to Say Farewell

Into this world with love she brought you, enduring all the pain;
She held you close in later years, when you cried tears like rain.

Like a lady and a mother she taught you how to be;
Guiding you along as you faced each new life mystery.

Some days you didn't get along and fought like cats and dogs;
But you always came back together with love, after endless
dialogues.

Always by your side she stood with you through thick and thin;
Never did she let you down, but taught you how to win.

So many memories of happy times together you did share;
You know in your heart that your mother was beyond compare.

Now her days are passing by quicker than we want to see;
You hear the doctor's diagnoses, but still you don't want to
believe.

You gather friends and family so that each may bid farewell;
Your emotions start going round and round like a runaway
carousel.

God gives us our parents, family and friends to love here for a
time;
Then one day He takes them home, without warning, reason or
rhyme.

Never pass up an opportunity to say I Love you every chance you
get;
You never know when it may be yours or their last sunset.

It won't be easy to say farewell when it's time for them to leave;
But remember that as Christians, together you'll spend
eternity.

Your tears will fall like a summer thunder storm of rain;
Just know that she is now happy and no longer in any pain.

The tears that you cry now are for the loneliness that you feel;
Just know that God is with you and your broken heart He will
heal.

Go forward each day doing the best that you can do;
Just know that she is looking down smiling with love on you.

In time the pain will loosen its grip on your heart my friend;
That will be another sign that your heart is beginning to mend.

Then it will be time to move on with your life and start again;
It's now time to step forward and let the true healing begin.

God bless you all that are going through suffering, loss and
pain;
I pray my humble words will in part, help you to sustain.

~~~

*He will swallow up death forever. The Sovereign Lord will wipe
away the tears from all faces;* Isaiah 25:8

That everyone who believes may have eternal life in him.
John 3:1

"Honor your father and mother" Ephesians 6:2

*He will wipe away every tear from their eyes, and death shall be
no more, neither shall there be mourning, nor crying, nor pain
anymore, for the former things have passed away."*
Revelation 21:4

*For everything there is a season, and a time for every matter
under heaven:* Ecclesiastes 3:1

Michael Gasaway

Legend of the Heavenly Oak

Inside the gates of heaven there is an old oak tree I'm told;
There it stands in its majesty so very stately and bold.

It awaits all that enter and gives them a place to reflect;
Some move quickly past, just simply choosing to forget.

Some leave yellow ribbons with loved ones names written upon;
They know they will find them, when it's their time to move on.

There are many benches under the spreading branches of this
heavenly tree;
Some are empty; others have a single person waiting for their
love to share eternity.

Sitting there waiting and wondering as each new group enters in;
Will this be the time that they get to begin again?

Patiently she has been waiting but does not know for how long;
For there is no night or day, there is just a heavenly song.

At times she wonders if he will recognize her when he does finally
arrive;
But she knows unlike some, that their love was true and destined
to survive.

Under the oak is where she said she would wait;
If the legend was true, the other would be there inside those
heavenly gates.

She felt him before she saw him enter, walking her way;
Rushing to greet him; glad the legend she did obey.

Like they had never been apart for even a day;
Now together they were again, and for all eternity to stay.

So if your love is true and to heaven you are both bound;
Whoever leaves first can wait under the oak to be found.

For if you were meant to be together for all eternity;
Then the other will be waiting just inside heaven's gate
under the heavenly oak tree.

~~~

"For God so loved the world, that he gave his only Son, that whoever believes in him should not perish but have eternal life."
John 3:16

He will wipe away every tear from their eyes, and death shall be no more, neither shall there be mourning, nor crying, nor pain anymore, for the former things have passed away.
Revelation 21:4

For if we live, we live to the Lord, and if we die, we die to the Lord. So then, whether we live or whether we die, we are the Lord's. Romans 14:8

"Let not your hearts be troubled. Believe in God; believe also in me. In my Father's house are many rooms. If it were not so, would I have told you that I go to prepare a place for you? And if I go and prepare a place for you, I will come again and will take you to myself, that where I am you may be also. And you know the way to where I am going."
John 14:1-4

Yes, we are of good courage, and we would rather be away from the body and at home with the Lord.
2 Corinthians 5:8

"O death, where is your victory? O death, where is your sting?" 1 Corinthians 15:55

Breakthrough

Put your faith and trust in God up above;
Then he will guide you with His perfect love.

The way may not be clear from what you now see;
Just keep trusting and praying to God that in His perfect will
you'll be.

Sometimes you have to go back in order to begin again;
Do it differently and get it right, in order to win.

In prayer keep, every step you take along the way;
Ask God to guide your steps and give you peace each day.

Don't let your pride and your own thoughts take you off course;
Keep praying and believing and remember He is the source.

Remember that what looks impossible to us or could never be;
To God is just a small task, another moment in eternity.

Today may be the day your answered prayers come true;
Just keep believing and know that God is listening to you.

When all hope seems to be gone and the light you cannot see;
God will reach down and whisper, "Just trust and follow me".

Cast your worries and cares aside and just believe;
He has a plan that one day soon you will achieve.

It's always darkest before the dawn and in the storms of life;
Just keep trusting and believing as He delivers you from this
strife.

This storm shall pass and the sun shall shine upon you once
again;
Know that He is always with you, just like a trusted friend.

Thank God for walking with you and showing you the way;
Never give up on your dreams and for them continue to pray.

It's not in our time that our dreams will come to pass;
But in Gods time, sometimes they come slow and sometimes
fast.

Nothing is too big or impossible that God cannot do;
Just keep praying, trusting and believing and you'll see your
breakthrough.

∾∾∾

*Jesus looked at them and said, "With man this is impossible,
but not with God; all things are possible with God."*
Mark 10:27

*Now faith is the assurance of things hoped for, the conviction of
things not seen.*
Hebrews 11:1

*Trust in the Lord with all your heart, and do not lean on your
own understanding.*
Proverbs 3:5

*When the Spirit of truth comes, he will guide you into all the
truth, for he will not speak on his own authority, but whatever he
hears he will speak, and he will declare to you the things that are
to come.*
John 16:13

*And whatever you ask in prayer, you will receive, if you have
faith.* Matthew 21:22

*The heart of man plans his way, but the Lord establishes his
steps.* Proverbs 16:9

Michael Gasaway

Win or Lose

What's meant to be doesn't happen by chance;
It's the choices you make during life's dance.

If it's meant to be, is one of the greatest lies the devil has
perpetrated on humanity;
The choices you make that truly decide your destiny.

Too many people try to blame others or even God above;
They say; "if it's meant to be", especially when it comes to love.

It's not a case of whether it's meant to be or not;
Sometimes people just give up on that which they sought.

Maybe it was someone else's choice that changed your true
course;
You now get to choose to be a victor or a victim with just
remorse.

God gave us all free will and the ability to choose;
You get to decide each day whether you win or lose.

Quit blaming yourself and others for the mistakes that were
made;
Put fear aside and follow your dreams, the price has already been
paid.

Never too late to change your life and really believe;
Your future is in your mind and will become what you perceive it
to be.

So dream on to the brighter days that lay ahead just down the
road;
You get to write your own story and say how it's told.

Choose wisely and pray daily for guidance from above;
Remember the words you speak in life will cause you pain or
love.

Speak words of faith, love, health, prosperity and happiness
each day.
Never give up on your dreams and remember, you are what
you say.

84

So take "If it's meant to be" and put it to rest;
This is your life and your choices will decide if you pass life's test.

~~~

This is the confidence we have in approaching God: that if we ask anything according to his will, he hears us. And if we know that he hears us—whatever we ask—we know that we have what we asked of him. 1 John 5:14-15

And let us not grow weary of doing good, for in due season we will reap, if we do not give up. Galatians 6:9

But you, take courage! Do not let your hands be weak, for your work shall be rewarded. 2 Chronicles 15:7

I have fought the good fight, I have finished the race, I have kept the faith. 2 Timothy 4:7

Be watchful, stand firm in the faith, act like men, be strong. Corinthians 16:13

I can do all things through him who strengthens me. Philippians 4:13

The heart of man plans his way, but the Lord establishes his steps. Proverbs 16:9

The steps of a man are established by the Lord, when he delights in his way; Psalm 37:23

Michael Gasaway

The Journey

Sometimes God leads us on a journey that we don't understand;
Just follow where He leads and let your heart and mind expand.

Keep trusting and believing each step that you take along the
way;
Put your faith and trust in God that everything will be OK.

This journey may take you to places that you have never been;
It may even take you back to places just to begin again.

Across the high mountains and to the valleys far below;
Just stay faithful as He shows you which way you should go.

You may face disappointments and struggles along the road;
When your burden gets too heavy, He will help you carry the
load.

One day He will open up your eyes so that you can really see;
That, which lies ahead of you, is a bright future and your destiny.

Always keep faithful and believe, with each new journey you
take;
Know that God always rides with you and you, He will never
forsake.

So have no fear and Cowboy up each and every day that you
live;
Grab hold life's reins and give it all you've got to give.

~~~

It is the Lord who goes before you. He will be with you; he will not leave you or forsake you. Do not fear or be dismayed.
Deuteronomy 31:8

Have I not commanded you? Be strong and courageous. Do not be frightened, and do not be dismayed, for the Lord your God is with you wherever you go.
Joshua 1:9

For I know the plans I have for you, declares the Lord, plans for welfare and not for evil, to give you a future and a hope.
Jeremiah 29:11

And after you have suffered a little while, the God of all grace, who has called you to his eternal glory in Christ, will himself restore, confirm, strengthen, and establish you.
1 Peter 5:10

And whatever you ask in prayer, you will receive, if you have faith.
Matthew 21:22

For still the vision awaits its appointed time; it hastens to the end—it will not lie. If it seems slow, wait for it; it will surely come; it will not delay. Habakkuk 2:3

Michael Gasaway

The Hawk

She saw it up there soaring through the sky high up above;
That hawk reminded her of God's perfect love.

There he was up on high, just soaring through the beautiful
spring sky;
Somehow she knew then that God would give her the strength to
get by.

So effortlessly that hawk soared through the crystal blue sky as
on she rode;
And she started feeling a peace that in time she knew would
grow.

This "road" she now found herself traveling was not her choice
alone;
Choices sometimes are made for us and take us far from home.

As she traveled on the loneliness seemed to creep in;
Hard as she tried not to, sometimes her thoughts they turned to
him.

Sometimes things happen in life and seem to be so unfair;
You want a hug, an encouraging word, to know that someone
does truly care.

In your spirit you seem to know that even through the pain that
you now feel;
That in due time even your broken heart, God will heal.

You just have to trust in God with all your might;
Hang on to his promise that in time it will, be all right.

Next time you see a hawk soaring high up above;
Just remember that God is always with you and ready to comfort
you with His unconditional love.

Keep your faith strong, look forward to what is yet to be;
Your best days are ahead of you, just trust God and
believe.

~~~

And we know that for those who love God all things work together for good, for those who are called according to his purpose.
Romans 8:28

Do not be anxious about anything, but in everything by prayer and supplication with thanksgiving let your requests be made known to God.
Philippians 4:6

Now may the Lord of peace himself give you peace at all times in every way. The Lord be with you all.
2 Thessalonians 3:16

Casting all your anxieties on him, because he cares for you. 1 Peter 5:7

The Lord is near to the brokenhearted and saves the crushed in spirit. Psalm 34:18

And whatever you ask in prayer, you will receive, if you have faith.
Matthew 21:22

For nothing will be impossible with God.
Luke 1:37

Now faith is the assurance of things hoped for, the conviction of things not seen.
Hebrews 11:1

Michael Gasaway

The Book

I never read it much but always kept one around;
Then one day I discovered that within its words, life's answers
could be found.

Many stories it holds and how so many can ring true;
Just reading one sometimes will pick you up when you are blue.

You can read of life and death and of wars both won and lost;
It tells the story of God's love and the price He paid for us on
the cross.

Some verses you may not understand or be able to comprehend;
But keep an open heart and He will reveal it all to you in the
end.

Now I try to read a little everyday so that I may understand His
will;
Sometimes after I read it, I just pray and remain quiet and still.

There were days I would play "Bible roulette' and just let it fall
and open wide;
Then God revealed to me, that it was better to know where to go
for my answers inside.

Today I study His word daily and continue in His word to grow;
So that one day for someone I can help show them which way to
go.

Read your Bible every chance that you get and always do your
best;
Just remember you never know when it will be your turn to pass
God's test.

~~~

For the word of God is living and active, sharper than any two-edged sword, piercing to the division of soul and of spirit, of joints and of marrow, and discerning the thoughts and intentions of the heart.
Hebrews 4:12

But he answered, "It is written, "'Man shall not live by bread alone, but by every word that comes from the mouth of God.'"
Matthew 4:4

Your word is a lamp to my feet and a light to my path.
Psalm 119:105

So shall my word be that goes out from my mouth; it shall not return to me empty, but it shall accomplish that which I purpose, and shall succeed in the thing for which I sent it.
Isaiah 55:11

All Scripture is breathed out by God and profitable for teaching, for reproof, for correction, and for training in righteousness, 2 Timothy 3:16

This Book of the Law shall not depart from your mouth, but you shall meditate on it day and night, so that you may be careful to do according to all that is written in it. For then you will make your way prosperous, and then you will have good success.
Joshua 1:8

Michael Gasaway

The Birds Sing

Every morning I sit on the deck with a cup of coffee in hand;
I just sit and watch another sunrise that is always so grand.

Up in the trees I can hear the birds with one another sing along:
A friend once told me that it was for God that the birds did sing
their song.

She said that they sing all day to praise God up above;
For all the things He gave them and for his love.

It seems they know even better than man;
It's all up to God above, and everything is all part of His plan.

These singing birds can teach us a lot about life;
Just flying and singing all day without any strife.

Never do they worry as they just fly all about;
Somehow they even survive the most severe drought.

They don't worry about what tomorrow may bring;
Each day they greet the same and just continue to sing.

Such wonderful songs they seem to sing each day;
We should all try to let go and let God in much the same way.

Oh how carefree they seem as they fly through the bright blue
sky;
Never do they worry or question, why God why?

So the next time you hear a bird sing its song;
Just remember to whom you and they both belong.

If God takes care of them so not a care or worry do they
see;
Then how much more will He do for you and me, if we just
believe?

~~~

92

Let everything that has breath praise the Lord! Praise the Lord!
Psalm 150:6

*Do not be anxious about anything, but in everything by prayer
and supplication with thanksgiving let your requests be made
known to God. And the peace of God, which surpasses all
understanding, will guard your hearts and your minds in Christ
Jesus.*
Philippians 4:6-7

Casting all your anxieties on him, because he cares for you.
1 Peter 5:7

*Therefore I tell you, do not be anxious about your life, what you
will eat or what you will drink, nor about your body, what you will
put on. Is not life more than food, and the body more than
clothing? Look at the birds of the air: they neither sow nor reap
nor gather into barns, and yet your heavenly Father feeds them.
Are you not of more value than they? And which of you by being
anxious can add a single hour to his span of life? And why are
you anxious about clothing? Consider the lilies of the field, how
they grow: they neither toil nor spin, yet I tell you, even
Solomon in all his glory was not arrayed like one of these.*
Matthew 6:25-34

Michael Gasaway

Second Chances

Many a rough time he'd seen in his life;
Most of his years were filled with heartache and strife.

His journey had taken him from town to town;
In his heart he really just wanted to be found.

The years and time had taken their toll;
Now again he wandered down this dark and lonesome road.

He wonders at times if he'll ever get another chance;
To prove himself, and join in at life's dance.

Sometimes things happen through no fault of your own;
And you're left cold and lonely in the midst of a raging storm.

God will lead you to where you need to be;
Even through the darkness when you can't see.

You can't give up and need to just keep pushing on;
Your next chance and brighter future could be rising with the
dawn.

Oh those changes can come at such a slow pace;
Then at times they come so fast it's as if you were in a race.

You must be open and yield first to God above;
Then He will show you the way with His unyielding love.

It took some time, but he found his new place in life;
A second chance he was given without all the strife.

Now he looks back on this long road he's traveled down;
He reaches out to others so that they too can be found.

So never give up or think of giving in;
Just look to God above and give it all to him.

Journey forth into this new life that you now see;
Help others along the way so that they too can believe.

Never forget the lessons that you learned along the way;
Thank God for walking with you each and every day.

~~~

Then Peter came up and said to him, "Lord, how often will my brother sin against me, and I forgive him? As many as seven times?" Jesus said to him, "I do not say to you seven times, but seventy times seven.
Matthew 18:21-22

But this I call to mind, and therefore I have hope: The steadfast love of the Lord never ceases; his mercies never come to an end; they are new every morning; great is your faithfulness.
Lamentations 3:21-23

"Remember not the former things, nor consider the things of old." Isaiah 43:18

When the righteous cry for help, the Lord hears and delivers them out of all their troubles. The Lord is near to the brokenhearted and saves the crushed in spirit. Many are the afflictions of the righteous, but the Lord delivers him out of them all. He keeps all his bones; not one of them is broken.
Psalm 34:17-20

Michael Gasaway

Reason, Season, Lifetime

It may be for a season that they came into our life to be;
And the reason you may never fully understand or clearly see.

It may be for a reason that your paths may have crossed;
They may have been the one to lead and guide you, when you were lost.

It may be for a lifetime that they have come into your life to stay;
And if that be the case, thank God each and every day.

He will never forsake you or give you more than you can bear;
Sometimes He provides us with that special someone who truly does care.

We never know who or why people cross our paths you see;
It may be an angel or just someone special sent to help you with your needs.

Everyone who into our lives did come;
Has somehow altered and helped us to fully blossom.

Some may have caused happiness or pain;
Still others brought true love and your life forever they did change.

Whatever the reason, the season or the lifetime that they spent;
Just know that they were all heaven sent.

For everyone who has come your way;
Have taught you about how to live life better each and every day.

They may have helped with the things that you needed to do;
Or they may have been the one to help pick you up when you were blue.

They may have just been there to help you with your pain;
Or taught you how to dance and smile in the rain.

So remember the next time someone into your life does appear;
It may be for you, or your time to help them with their
fear.

So be ready and ever vigilant each day;
It may be your time to help guide someone lost down
"Life's Highway".

∼∼∼

*For everything there is a season, and a time for every matter
under heaven: a time to be born, and a time to die; a time to
plant, and a time to pluck up what is planted; a time to kill, and a
time to heal; a time to break down, and a time to build up; a
time to weep, and a time to laugh; a time to mourn, and a time
to dance; a time to cast away stones, and a time to gather
stones together; a time to embrace, and a time to refrain from
embracing;*
Ecclesiastes 3:1-8

*Two are better than one, because they have a good reward for
their toil. For if they fall, one will lift up his fellow. But woe to him
who is alone when he falls and has not another to lift him up!
Again, if two lie together, they keep warm, but how can one keep
warm alone?*
Ecclesiastes 4:9–11

Michael Gasaway

Never Give Up

When your days are gloomy and your fate you cannot see;
Just remember that with you, He will always be.

Lift up a prayer for guidance from heaven up above;
Then you will feel God's mercy and His eternal love.

He will never forsake you and with you He will always be;
Even in your darkest moments when you cannot feel Him or see.

For if He brings you to it, He will surely see you through it to the
end;
As He never takes you anywhere, He hasn't already been.

There is no obstacle He cannot overcome or task too hard to do;
No pain too great, that He won't be there to see you through.

Although the trials you're facing may seem like the roughest of
your life;
Remember with Him, you can face any strife.

In Him you will always have a trusted friend;
And on Him you can always count and forever depend.

When your days are gloomy and your fate you cannot see;
Just remember that with you, He will always be.

Just when you feel you can't take another step or move on;
Your heart's desire could be waiting over the horizon, rising with
the dawn.

So Never Give Up or think of giving in;
When your darkest hour approaches, just remember, turn to
Him.

~~~

But those who hope in the LORD will renew their strength. They will soar on wings like eagles; they will run and not grow weary, they will walk and not be faint.
Isaiah 40:31

Delight thyself also in the LORD; and he shall give thee the desires of thine heart.
Psalms 37:4

I can do all things through him who strengthens me.
Philippians 4:13

And let us not grow weary of doing good, for in due season we will reap, if we do not give up.
Galatians 6:9

And we know that for those who love God all things work together for good, for those who are called according to his purpose.
Romans 8:28

For I know the plans I have for you, declares the Lord, plans for welfare and not for evil, to give you a future and a hope.
Jeremiah 29:11

"But you, take courage! Do not let your hands be weak, for your work shall be rewarded."
2 Chronicles 15:7

Michael Gasaway

Life's Highway

The mysteries of God I do not understand nor do I try to
comprehend;
I just know that His word will prevail until the very end.

Sometime it's so hard to let go and Let God as some people say;
But I know that if I trust in Him, then better I will become each
day.

Over and over I used to ponder the troubles in my mind;
How will God work things out, but I know now, that He will in His
own time.

When it seemed that I couldn't go on another day with the
burden I carried within;
Then I was reminded that in his word it said, "Give it all to Him".

Don't worry about what tomorrow may bring;
Just lift up your eyes toward heaven and a praise song, sing.

Open your heart to Him who sits in heaven up above;
Then you will begin to feel His mercy and unconditional total
love.

His love will surround you and fill you so completely by both
night and day;
He will lead, guide and direct your steps showing you the way.

You should not despair or ever think of giving in;
He is always with you and on Him you can always depend.

Never alone will you ever be as by your side He will always
stand;
And when you can't seem to go on, He will carry you, just like
the foot prints in the sand.

So thank God as you wake each and every day;
For all the many blessings He's given you, and for walking
with you down,
"Life's Highway".

~~~

Therefore do not worry about tomorrow, for tomorrow will worry about itself. Each day has enough trouble of its own.
Matthew 6:34

But Jesus looked at them and said to them, "With men this is impossible, but with God all things are possible."
Matthew 19:26

Trust in the Lord with all your heart, and do not lean on your own understanding. In all your ways acknowledge him, and he will make straight your paths.
Proverbs 3:5-6

Cast your burden on the Lord, and he will sustain you; he will never permit the righteous to be moved.
Psalm 55:22

Give thanks in all circumstances; for this is the will of God in Christ Jesus for you.
1 Thessalonians 5:18

And let us not grow weary of doing good, for in due season we will reap, if we do not give up.
Galatians 6:9

Michael Gasaway

Hope You'll Bring

His father was never around much as he grew through the years;
Many a night he cried himself to sleep through a waterfall of
tears.

He never knew a father's love or felt his warm embrace;
To him and that little boy within, love really had a special place.

There was no father figure for him to look up to and try to be;
Slowly the years went by and he turned to his peers and the
street to see.

Now he travels the streets of life feeling so empty inside;
Sometimes he looks up to the sky and asks, Why God why?

Over the years he tried to fill the gaping hole he felt deep within;
He tried booze, drugs and sex to try and fill that hole in.

He had left two small children behind along with a wife;
Life's daily pressures were too much for him along with all the
strife.

Nothing seemed to ease the ache he felt deep within his heart
and soul;
Now he was just like his father had been to him, so long ago.

So the cycle repeats itself once again and another young man's
fate seems sealed;
When will it all change, when will they realize what's truly special
and real.

It's never too late to be the kind of father you never had;
You can break the cycle and make a difference by really being a
dad.

Stand up today and be the man that your father never was to
you;
Ask for God's help to guide you and he will see you through.

You still have time to go back and do the right thing;
It may be hard to do but in the end into a young man's life, hope
you'll bring.

Today in America we have too many young men with no father
figure at home;
They are left to be raised by a mother or grandmother and
feel so lost and alone.

Send up a prayer with me to all those young men, that
God will show them the way;
May He direct their steps and show them back home one
day.

~~~

*Now then, my children listen to me; blessed are those who keep
my ways. Listen to my instruction and be wise; do not disregard
it. Proverbs 8:32-33*

*Train up a child in the way he should go; and when he is old, he
will not depart from it. Proverbs 22:6*

*But they who wait for the Lord shall renew their strength; they
shall mount up with wings like eagles; they shall run and not be
weary; they shall walk and not faint.
Isaiah 40:31*

*Trust in the Lord with all your heart, and do not lean on your own
understanding. Proverbs 3:5*

*Father of the fatherless and protector of widows is God in his holy
habitation. Psalm 68:5*

Michael Gasaway

Footprints in the Sand

When you are feeling so alone and can't seem to stand;
Remember those footprints in the sand.

Sometimes in life you have to let go;
So that God can teach you, that which will help you to grow.

The lessons always come with a price you have to pay;
But no higher than Jesus paid to show us the way.

Remember that you are never truly alone;
And that He also carries you when you can't go on.

When you feel like giving up, just lift your arms and say;
"I give it all to you Dear Lord, take this pain away."

It may take some time for you to see;
As the teaching and testing may not be done completely.

So don't give up or give in;
Just remember that you have already turned it over to Him.

He will never give you more than you can handle they say;
Just ask God to make it one more day.

Then make that day the best one yet;
You may not remember but you will never forget.

Never will He forsake you or leave you alone, and in the end;
There He'll be, to carry you home.

Live your life the best that you can;
Always seek Him and remember those footprints in the sand.

~~~

"It is the Lord who goes before you. He will be with you; he will not leave you or forsake you. Do not fear or be dismayed."
Deuteronomy 31:8

For nothing will be impossible with God.
Luke 1:37

For I know the plans I have for you, declares the Lord, plans for welfare and not for evil, to give you a future and a hope.
Jeremiah 29:11

And we know that for those who love God all things work together for good, for those who are called according to his purpose.
Romans 8:28

Rejoice always, pray without ceasing, give thanks in all circumstances; for this is the will of God in Christ Jesus for you.
1 Thessalonians 5:16-18

And without faith it is impossible to please him, for whoever would draw near to God must believe that he exists and that he rewards those who seek him.
Hebrews 11:6

Michael Gasaway

Sometimes

Sometimes things don't go quite as you planned;
That's when you must remember the foot prints in the sand.

Keep trusting in His perfect unconditional love;
It is He that will guide your steps from above.

Don't lose your joy or your faith along the way;
Now is the time to hit your knees and really pray.

Pray for His guidance and direction from up on high;
He will catch each and every tear that you cry.

Some days won't go as we intended or hoped they would;
Just keep living your life as you know you should.

Live each day the best that you can and always do what's right;
The darkness will always fade, followed by the morning's light.

It always seems darkest before dawn or your blessings come;
Just never give up and one day your future will be in full
blossom.

Blossom forth it will, as you could never have imagined or
believed;
Your dreams, desires and plans and more, you will achieve.

So just keep believing and trusting in God's mighty word;
Give Him all your doubts and fears, they have already been
conquered.

It's not always easy, but keep trying to find joy in all that you do;
This will let God know; you're trusting in Him and being true.

~~~

Commit to the L*ORD* *whatever you do, and he will establish your plans.*
Proverbs 16:3

In their hearts humans plan their course, but the L*ORD* *establishes their steps.*
Proverbs 16:9

And we know that for those who love God all things work together for good, for those who are called according to his purpose
Romans 8:28

And let us not grow weary of doing good, for in due season we will reap, if we do not give up
Galatians 6:9

Trust in the Lord with all your heart, and do not lean on your own understanding. In all your ways acknowledge him, and he will make straight your paths.
Proverbs 3:5-6

I will instruct you and teach you in the way you should go; I will counsel you with my eye upon you.
Psalm 32:8

"Behold, God is my salvation; I will trust, and will not be afraid; for the Lord God is my strength and my song, and he has become my salvation."
Isaiah 12:2

Michael Gasaway

Feelings

A friend once told me that you should never bury your feelings
alive;
They will never die but only surface again, leaving you wondering
why.

So don't just bury those feeling that you once had;
It doesn't matter how bad they were, or that they made you sad.

Each feeling has to be dealt with and put to rest;
It will not be easy, but it's something you must do, to pass life's
test.

Explore each feeling that still makes you sad or mad;
Then ask yourself why you still feel that way, instead of being
glad.

The past can't be changed from what it has become;
You must just learn from it, accept it, move on and be done.

It does no use to ignore it or try to continue to blame;
All you're really doing in the end is fanning a flickering flame.

Yes, some things can be changed or fixed with time;
But that normally only comes with forgiveness, and the changing
of minds.

Forgiveness, however, is a good place for you to begin this;
Start off by forgiving yourself, and then anyone else on the list.

Why do you have to forgive yourself you may ask?
It's just part of the process and the only way you can truly let go
of the past.

Past feelings are like that weed that seems even in winter to
grow;
Nothing around it seems alive, but there's that weed, just
growing so bold.

That weed may even come with its own beauty as many
often do;
But the roots are as deep as the pain down inside of you.

Like those weeds that just seem to keep on growing;
You can't kill them and be rid of them with just a top cut mowing.

You have to dig them up, root and all way down deep;
Just like those feelings you buried alive and unknowingly decided to keep.

Once those feelings are pulled up by the roots at last;
Then you can begin healing and finally be free of your past.

Then you can plant new seeds of love in this good ground;
Then the beauty that blossoms won't be surrounded by weeds growing all around.

So start today as you don't have a moment to waste;
It's your turn to get back out there, start living again, and to WIN at life's race.

∿∿∿

Be kind to one another, tenderhearted, forgiving one another, as God in Christ forgave you. Ephesians 4:32

And we know that for those who love God all things work together for good, for those who are called according to his purpose. Romans 8:28

Know this, my beloved brothers: let every person be quick to hear, slow to speak, slow to anger; for the anger of man does not produce the righteousness of God. James 1:19-20

Let all bitterness and wrath and anger and clamor and slander be put away from you, along with all malice. Ephesians 4:31

Blessed is the man who remains steadfast under trial, for when he has stood the test he will receive the crown of life, which God has promised to those who love him. James 1:12

Michael Gasaway

True Treasure

When two hearts find each other and they become one;
They have found true treasure that is second to none.

For true treasure does not really apply to money and things;
It applies to true love, between two that makes your heart sing.

You were created to love and be loved by one special other;
Everyone goes through life searching trying to discover.

Don't let the trials and strife of everyday life, take you off course;
Your one true love may be waiting for you at the source.

Don't let that diamond you hold slip through your hands;
While you're sifting through the grains of shifting sands.

Hold on tight but with a gentle touch of love;
Ask for God to guide your steps from heaven above.

May your heart be receptive and open when love does knock;
Don't let fear and your past become your stumbling block.

Yes, true treasure is hard to find in this world of strife;
Keep your heart open and be ever vigilant as you pass through
life.

May God open your eyes to truly see and give you an open mind;
This I pray, that your true love treasure, you will realize in time.

~~~

For where your treasure is, there will your heart be also.
Luke 12:34

An excellent wife who can find? She is far more precious than jewels. The heart of her husband trusts in her, and he will have no lack of gain. She does him good, and not harm, all the days of her life. Proverbs 31:10-12

So now faith, hope, and love abide, these three; but the greatest of these is love. 1 Corinthians 13:13

Love is patient and kind; love does not envy or boast; it is not arrogant or rude. It does not insist on its own way; it is not irritable or resentful; it does not rejoice at wrongdoing, but rejoices with the truth. Love bears all things, believes all things, hopes all things, endures all things. Love never ends. As for prophecies, they will pass away; as for tongues, they will cease; as for knowledge, it will pass away. 1 Corinthians 13:4-8

Let all that you do be done in love. 1 Corinthians 16:14

Anyone who does not love does not know God, because God is love. 1 John 4:8

And above all these put on love, which binds everything together in perfect harmony. Colossians 3:14

Beloved, let us love one another, for love is from God, and whoever loves has been born of God and knows God. 1 John 4:7

We love because he first loved us. 1 John 4:19

Michael Gasaway

The Story

She wasn't sure when, but inside she knew that her story had to
be told;
Conflicted emotions rose inside, as she wondered if after
listening, he just might go.

Better now than later she thought, it had to be done;
By tonight she knew her answer would come.

So there they sat with soft music playing so soft and low;
The candle flames flickered and made the room all aglow.

Feeling that the mood was set and this was the night;
Now it was time to tell her story and to start things off right.

Her story started back at the beginning, even before;
Of life she spoke and took him through each of her life's doors.

He listened so intently not interrupting except to give her a
gentle kiss;
She wondered if this would be the last time she felt his lips.

The hours went by as the story of her life began to unfold;
Sometimes she glanced at his reaction to what he had just been
told.

By the stories from our past and what we learn with each passing
day;
It's these life lessons that help us grow and make it down 'Life's
Highway'.

At times it takes someone special in our lives for the story to be
told;
Then other times it's through telling our story that heals us and
makes us whole.

Our lives are made up from the many stories of our past;
A few come with heart ache and pain and of the love that didn't
last.

Some of those stories put a song in our heart and some
bring a smile to our face;

As we remember back to how we felt God's wonderful and
amazing grace.

The truth will always find its way even from the darkest
abyss;
So build your relationship on honesty, and then there will
never be a last kiss.

We all have a story and its best to be honest and up front if
you want love to grow;
Now theirs is not a story of the past or what was, but now a
story of love yet to unfold.

~~~

And you will know the truth, and the truth will set you free.
John 8:32

Pray for us, for we are sure that we have a clear conscience,
desiring to act honorably in all things. Hebrews 13:18

Let all that you do be done in love. 1 Corinthians 16:14

Above all, keep loving one another earnestly, since love covers a
multitude of sins. 1 Peter 4:8

Sanctify them in the truth; your word is truth. John 17:17

Stand therefore, having fastened on the belt of truth, and having
put on the breastplate of righteousness, Ephesians 6:14

Lying lips are an abomination to the Lord, but those who act
faithfully are his delight. Proverbs 12:22

The sum of your word is truth, and every one of your righteous
rules endures forever. Psalm 119:160

Michael Gasaway

The Climb

Standing on the deck they watched the Frio River rush by far
below;
Inside each was feeling a peace and maybe love that in time
might grow.

Beyond the rushing river the mountain rose high against the
deep blue fall sky;
Looking into her striking green eyes, he smiled and said, "Let's
give that mountain a try".

Holding hands they waded across the Frio feeling the cold water
as it rushed by;
Leading the way they slowly started their ascent up the steep
and rugged mountain side.

They seemed to bond even closer with each obstacle and every
level they did climb;
Just one look into their eyes and you could see a new love
starting for each that was so sublime.

Reaching high above, they then turned and looked at the
sparkling river and the green valley beyond;
Holding each other close for a long while and then they continued
to climb on.

Along the way she fell and scraped her leg and started to bleed;
Kneeling down he gently kissed the blood away from her skinned
knee.

He removed the bandanna from his neck and tied it tenderly
around her leg;
Then he helped her up, she kissed him softly but had nothing to
say.

She had been taken back by the chivalrous deed that she had
just seen;
Now she was wondering if this really was just some romantic
dream.

The journey down was even harder than had been the ascent;
But something seemed to have happened up on that mountain
that was heaven sent.

Yes something special happened to them as they climbed
that mountain high;
A Love for each other seemed to blossom and grow with each
and every stride.

At the bottom he picked a lavender wildflower and placed it
in her hair;
Gently she touched his face looking deep into his eyes and
said, "I'm there".

Fear was banished from their lives on that beautiful Texas fall
day;
Forward into tomorrow they now go together in love with God
leading their way.

Never give up on love as you never know where true love may
shine;
Just keep trusting in God and believing in His grand design.

~~~

Let all that you do be done in love. 1 Corinthians 16:14

*And above all these put on love, which binds everything together
in perfect harmony. Colossians 3:14*

*And whatever you ask in prayer, you will receive, if you have
faith." Matthew 21:22*

*So now faith, hope, and love abide, these three; but the greatest
of these is love. 1 Corinthians 13:13*

*And we know that for those who love God all things work
together for good, for those who are called according to his
purpose. Romans 8:28*

115

Michael Gasaway

Still in Love

She saw them in the distance walking down the beach hand n
hand;
It was an older couple walking at sunset through the sand.

Her thoughts were of the struggles and the joys of life they had
each seen;
And still together through it all, it painted in her mind such a
wonderful scene.

What a beautiful sight to see, such a display of love and
devotion;
That is what she yearned for and prayed each night to God in
anticipation.

There was not a more beautiful picture of love to see in her
mind;
She knew in her heart that this older couple had been blessed
divine.

Little did she know of the many struggles they had each seen in
their day?
How once they had even parted and gone their separate ways.

But true love, determination and God's guidance from up on
high;
Had brought them back together as husband and wife His will to
exemplify.

You never know the stories or difficulties that people endure
through life;
Everyone faces obstacles, challenges and sometimes emotional
strife.

So keep believing and put your prayers and faith in God high
above;
That one day you may be walking along that beach hand 'n hand
at 85, still in love.

~~~

116

For through wisdom your days will be many, and years will be added to your life.
Proverbs 9:1

And above all these put on love, which binds everything together in perfect harmony.
Colossians 3:14

Beloved, let us love one another, for love is from God, and whoever loves has been born of God and knows God.
1 John 4:7

And whatever you ask in prayer, you will receive, if you have faith.
Matthew 21:22

And let us consider how to stir up one another to love and good works, not neglecting to meet together, as is the habit of some, but encouraging one another, and all the more as you see the Day drawing near.
Hebrews 10:24-25

Love is patient and kind; love does not envy or boast; it is not arrogant or rude. It does not insist on its own way; it is not irritable or resentful; it does not rejoice at wrongdoing, but rejoices with the truth. Love bears all things, believes all things, hopes all things, endures all things.
1 Corinthians 13:4-7

Above all, keep loving one another earnestly, since love covers a multitude of sins.
1 Peter 4:8

Michael Gasaway

Prisoner of Fear

The little girl that existed within her had lived in fear most of her
life;
This was a fear from all her years of emotional strife.

She never knew true unconditional love or a Mother's loving
embrace;
To her and that little girl within, love never really had a special
place.

The words; I Love You, were never really spoken in a meaningful
loving way;
To her they were just emotionless words with no deep meaning
to convey.

A failed marriage and broken trust only deepened her pain
inside;
Her fear and worries were now in control and would become her
guide.

Worries, fear and anger stole the joy and happiness she found for
awhile;
Now, on she goes just getting by, instead of that walk down the
aisle.

Walls she built as the years drifted by like the clouds she
watched above;
At times she tried to reach out, and sometimes even sought
God's love.

Time and years took their toll and a prisoner of fear she became;
Fear of love or a lack of love created within her a heart gone
lame.

Never did she gain the ability to really give her heart and love to
a man;
Once upon a time she came close but fear overtook her and off
she ran.

Now alone she drifts through life and wonders why love has
left her emotionally blind;
She so wanted to be able to give real love, the never ending
unconditional kind.

You can never truly give unconditional love to another if fear is in
control of your life;
Try as you may, the end will always come, caused by your
emotional strife.

So open up your heart to God up above and ask Him to take
your fear away;
Then walk into tomorrow and for you I pray, a new beginning
and a bright new day.

~~~

*Fear not, for I am with you; be not dismayed, for I am your
God; I will strengthen you, I will help you, I will uphold you with
my righteous right hand.
Isaiah 41:10*

*There is no fear in love, but perfect love casts out fear. For fear
has to do with punishment, and whoever fears has not been
perfected in love.
1 John 4:18*

*I sought the Lord, and he answered me and delivered me from all
my fears. Psalm 34:4*

*The fear of man lays a snare, but whoever trusts in the Lord is
safe. Proverbs 29:25*

*Do not be anxious about anything, but in everything by prayer
and supplication with thanksgiving let your requests be made
known to God.
Philippians 4:6*

Michael Gasaway

Doubts and Fears

Forgive me Lord for my doubts and all of my fears;
I know that all of my petitions and prayers you do hear.

Sometimes I don't recall the prayers you answered from my
past;
But then I remember, that my even my dreams you did surpass.

Now I sit patiently and wait upon you again dear Lord;
In my heart I know that all that was lost, will be restored.

It's not easy to wait patiently, this I know to be true;
But patient I must be, with my complete trust in you.

I know that your timing and mine are not always the same;
But your timing is always perfect and your glory I will proclaim.

So, on I go down this road and thank you each night and day;
One day soon my heart's desire you will fulfill, I pray.

Thank you God for being faithful to your word that in the Bible I
read;
I know my answered prayer is over the horizon, just ahead.

Shout for joy will I, and praise your name to all that will hear;
I was faithful as was God, and there never was a reason to doubt
or fear.

~~~

*When doubts filled my mind, your comfort gave me renewed
hope and cheer.
Psalm 94:19*

*For God has not given us a spirit of fear and timidity, but of
power, love, and self-discipline.
2 Timothy 1:7*

*And he said to them, "Why are you troubled, and why do doubts
arise in your hearts?
Luke 24:38*

*Now faith is the assurance of things hoped for, the conviction of
things not seen.
Hebrews 11:1*

*So faith comes from hearing, and hearing through the word of
Christ.
Romans 10:17*

*I can do all things through him who strengthens me.
Philippians 4:13*

*Delight yourself in the Lord, and he will give you the desires of
your heart.
Psalm 37:4*

Michael Gasaway

Do What's Right

The tears fell from her eyes like the leaves from the trees;
Her hopes and dreams faded away on the autumn breeze.

Somehow he had gotten through the walls she had built around
her heart;
Down this road again, she had sworn that she would never start.

It had seemed so real as if delivered from God up above;
This was the one she felt, the one she would forever love.

He had said all the right words and made it all seem so real;
But the lies he had told in the end had broken the seal.

Why can't people just be honest and do what's right;
Now alone she sits and wonders why, into another lonely night.

She questions herself and if true everlasting love is really real;
It will take some time for her broken heart to heal.

This is a story that in today's world is all too very true;
Both men and women are just as guilty of breaking this rule in
two.

It all comes down to doing what is right in the eyes of God
above;
Always search your heart and do what's right for real
unconditional love.

Cheating, lying and causing another person any pain;
This in the end will only leave you both crying tears like rain.

So always do what is right and with love in your heart;
Treat one another with love and respect from the very start.

Don't give up on love and that it will come your way;
Just keep trusting and believing, and each day continue to
pray.

∾∾∾

Do what is right and good in the Lord's sight....
Deuteronomy 6:18

Therefore to him that knoweth to do good, and doeth [it] not,
to him it is sin.
James 4:17

Wherefore, my beloved brethren, let every man be swift to
hear, slow to speak, slow to wrath:
James 1:19

Let him kiss me with the kisses of his mouth: for thy love is
better than wine.
Song of Solomon 1:2

Let love be without dissimulation. Abhor that which is evil;
cleave to that which is good.
Romans 12:9

Love is patient, love is kind. It does not envy, it does not boast,
it is not proud. It does not dishonor others, it is not self-seeking,
it is not easily angered, it keeps no record of wrongs. Love does
not delight in evil but rejoices with the truth. It always protects,
always trusts, always hopes, always perseveres. Love never fails.
1 Corinthians 13:4-8

Michael Gasaway

Come Together and Pray

It's always the first casualty whether it is in love or war;
Always first to close is that particular door.

Most of the time it's not with intent or malice in mind;
You just reach an impasse and find your thoughts are no longer aligned.

Neither seems to see or understand what is happening at the time;
But slowly everything just seems to begin to unwind.

People can always look back and see when it started to fade;
But at the time, their hearts desire was never really conveyed.

I speak of communication between nations, but mostly of two people who share their love;
It seems to start failing, when we stop praying to God above.

Hurt feelings, anger, resentment or just not understanding can lead to this end;
But without open communication, there is no place to begin again.

So open your mind and heart to God up above;
Pray that He always leads your communication with His purpose and love.

Never stop talking and really hearing what the other person has to say;
You may both just need to come together and pray.

Pray that God opens your hearts and minds to the others point of view;
Understand that this is never the time to just sit and argue.

Be open and honest about your true feelings and what you really need;
This is the time for both to come together and let God intercede.

Ask God to choose your words and the meaning they need to imply;

Let your hearts be open, so that in the end your soul, God will
satisfy.

I pray for all, that your words always come from God, through
your heart;
Let God lead your steps as it's never too late to start.

Begin today with a door that may have been closed by words
that were never spoken;
Let God guide you so that His words and meaning are certain.

Thank God for helping you to choose the words you need to
use;
May God lead and guide you always to your divine
breakthroughs.

∾∾∾

*Know this, my beloved brothers: let every person be quick to
hear, slow to speak, slow to anger; James 1:19*

*Let no corrupting talk come out of your mouths, but only such as
is good for building up, as fits the occasion, that it may give
grace to those who hear. Ephesians 4:29*

*Set a guard, O Lord, over my mouth; keep watch over the door
of my lips! Psalm 141:3*

*The tongue of the wise commends knowledge, but the mouths of
fools pour out folly. Proverbs 15:2*

*Let no corrupting talk come out of your mouths, but only such as
is good for building up, as fits the occasion, that it may give
grace to those who hear. Ephesians 4:29*

Michael Gasaway

Choices

Life is all about choices they say;
The ones we make, we will live with for all of our days.

When a choice you have to make, look for guidance from up
above;
Pray that you will always make it with unselfish love.

You never know what the choice you make may bring;
It could mean heartache and pain or maybe a gold ring.

These choices you make today will affect all your tomorrows yet
to be;
So when a choice you must make, choose ever so wisely.

Sometimes you have time to ponder and pray which choice you
should make;
Then there are times choices are made for you, and decide your
fate.

Choices are the free will God gave you from the start;
Make each choice with love, deep from in your heart.

Choose your tomorrows the best that you can;
You really do hold your future in the palm of your hand.

Now press your palms together and do really pray;
'God guide me and direct the choices that I make each and every
day.'

~~~

The heart of man plans his way, but the Lord establishes his steps.
Proverbs 16:9

How much better to get wisdom than gold! To get understanding is to be chosen rather than silver.
Proverbs 16:16

Trust in the Lord with all your heart, and do not lean on your own understanding. In all your ways acknowledge him, and he will make straight your paths.
Proverbs 3:5-6

I will instruct you and teach you in the way you should go; I will counsel you with my eye upon you.
Psalm 32:8

No temptation has overtaken you that is not common to man. God is faithful, and he will not let you be tempted beyond your ability, but with the temptation he will also provide the way of escape, that you may be able to endure it.
1 Corinthians 10:13

Michael Gasaway

Don't Misuse It

It's given easy by some and they hope and pray for the best;
With others you will have to pass their special test.

Others believe that over time it has to be earned;
Then there are those that are afraid that they'll just once again
get burned.

Some say it's hard to do because of what's in their past;
And with others they just can't believe that it will last.

This was once something that was so highly prized by man;
Once it was as common as grains of sand.

This was supposed to be how you led your life;
It was something special between friends but especially husband
and wife.

Now it's not as common as it was in times past;
But when you find it between two, pray that it will always last.

All seem to agree on this one fact;
When it's broken or lost, it's hard and nearly impossible to ever
get back.

TRUST, is what I speak of in these words and rhyme;
Yours freely to give and receive don't misuse it, when it's your
time.

~~~

Not a word from their mouth can be trusted; their heart is filled with malice. Their throat is an open grave; with their tongues they tell lies.
Psalm 5:9

Whoever speaks the truth gives honest evidence, but a false witness utters deceit.
Proverbs 12:17

Righteous lips are the delight of a king, and he loves him who speaks what is right.
Proverbs 16:13

Lying lips are an abomination to the Lord, but those who act faithfully are his delight.
Proverbs 12:22

Better is a poor person who walks in his integrity than one who is crooked in speech and is a fool.
Proverbs 19:1

For we aim at what is honorable not only in the Lord's sight but also in the sight of man.
2 Corinthians 8:21

A dishonest man spreads strife, and a whisperer separates close friends.
Proverbs 16:28

Michael Gasaway

Communication

You can speak without saying a word;
But it is seldom ever heard.

Your actions can speak volumes and say much;
Especially when followed by a gentle touch.

Communication takes many forms its true;
Such as a smile that says; I Love You.

Sometimes silence speaks the loudest still;
This may leave you with a cold chill.

Listen with your soul and heart;
So you can feel the words that they impart.

Always listen to understand and learn;
Not just to reply when it's your turn.

Forever be honest in what you speak;
Love and truth you should always seek.

Face to face talking is always the best;
Sometimes modern forms just fail the test.

Body language and expressions can convey many things;
They can show you one's true inner feelings.

Look for truth deep within their eyes;
As it's been said, the eyes never lie.

As you can see communication comes in many ways;
Use them all and you, it will amaze.

Let God lead you in what you hear and say;
And then your understanding and words will never stray.

~~~

Let no corrupting talk come out of your mouths, but only such as is good for building up, as fits the occasion, that it may give grace to those who hear.
Ephesians 4:29

Gracious words are like a honeycomb, sweetness to the soul and health to the body.
Proverbs 16:24

Let your speech always be gracious, seasoned with salt, so that you may know how you ought to answer each person.
Colossians 4:6

Know this, my beloved brothers: let every person be quick to hear, slow to speak, slow to anger;
James 1:19

A soft answer turns away wrath, but a harsh word stirs up anger.
Proverbs 15:1

Truthful lips endure forever, but a lying tongue is but for a moment. Proverbs 12:19

"One who is faithful in a very little is also faithful in much, and one who is dishonest in a very little is also dishonest in much.
Luke 16:10

Michael Gasaway

It's More Than Just a Word

It's the most misused word in any language today;
Many people use it, but then just throw it away.

This word should be held higher than most any other;
Hollow and empty is the word many soon discover.

Too many people say it with ease and really no meaning to
impart;
A few like me only ever say it, from the heart.

The Bible explains what love means and is so easy to read;
Why then do so many people refuse the words to heed?

So precious is this wonderful gift from God above;
Why do so many people misuse this word called love?

Some just confuse love with other emotions in life;
But real true love will stand together against any strife.

Love is not something to be used and then discarded when times
get tough;
Real true love never fails, even when times get rough.

Next time before you use this word and its true meaning to
convey;
Read what it says in the Bible and what God's word does say.

Then only say it with true meaning from your heart as the Bible
does imply;
God then will bless your love as His gift to you, because Him you
did glorify.

~~~

*And now these three remain: faith, hope and love. But the
greatest of these is love.
1 Corinthians 13:13*

*A glad heart makes a cheerful face, but by sorrow of heart the
spirit is crushed.
Proverbs 15:13*

*Let all that you do be done in love.
1 Corinthians 16:14*

*Anyone who does not love does not know God, because God is
love.
1 John 4:8*

*And above all these put on love, which binds everything together
in perfect harmony.
Colossians 3:14*

*Beloved, let us love one another, for love is from God, and
whoever loves has been born of God and knows God.
1 John 4:7*

Michael Gasaway

Love and Money

Worries about money seemed to always be on her troubled mind;
About the future she worried and thought of, time after time.

Her faith and belief was not strong enough to guide her way;
True feeling and thoughts, she never really conveyed.

Security about the future was on her mind night and day;
The love she felt for him, wasn't enough to make her stay.

She decided to choose money over love this time around;
Thinking that was where her security and happiness could be
found.

The seasons slowly passed by and the leaves fell from the trees;
Now alone and lonely she sits feeling the cold winter breeze.

Only true love can warm your soul and ease your troubled heart;
God gave us free will and your choices are up to you from the
start.

No, Money can't buy you that special hand to hold;
Or wipe away the tears as you both grow old.

True love is the only thing that will watch over you when you're
sick at night;
It's real unconditional love that will hold you close and feels so
right.

If it's between love and money that is your choice to make;
Pray to God above that the right road you take.

I've seen many an unhappy person with money to burn;
But true unconditional love lasts forever and is always returned.

May you find your one true love that will light up your life;
I pray that God will bless you and guide you through life's
strife.

Money and love make the world go round some people say;
But about money you won't be thinking on your dying day.

~~~

Love is patient and kind; love does not envy or boast; it is not arrogant or rude. It does not insist on its own way; it is not irritable or resentful; it does not rejoice at wrongdoing, but rejoices with the truth. Love bears all things, believes all things, hopes all things, endures all things. Love never ends. As for prophecies, they will pass away; as for tongues, they will cease; as for knowledge, it will pass away.
1 Corinthians 13:4-8

Let all that you do be done in love.
1 Corinthians 16:14

And above all these put on love, which binds everything together in perfect harmony.
Colossians 3:14

Keep your life free from love of money, and be content with what you have, for he has said, "I will never leave you nor forsake you."
Hebrews 13:5

For the love of money is a root of all kinds of evils. It is through this craving that some have wandered away from the faith and pierced themselves with many pangs.
1 Timothy 6:10

He who loves money will not be satisfied with money, nor he who loves wealth with his income; this also is vanity.
Ecclesiastes 5:10

Michael Gasaway

I Am Blessed

I am blessed in my misery or experiencing life's best;
Your future depends on how you face each of life's tests.

Life is not always full of sunshine and happy days;
Sometimes you must remain faithful even through misery's haze.

Keep your eye on the prize that lies within your heart;
Keep trusting in God and each day, do your part.

Your part is to pray and have faith in God's power above;
Believe, no matter the outcome you'll be blessed with God's love.

Acceptance of Gods will is not always an easy thing to do;
But trust you must as He knows best and will show His love to
you.

Pray each day for the desires of your heart, that lies within;
Know that your prayers will be answered, and then begin.

Begin this new day that God has opened your heart to receive;
Now go live your life so that through you, God, others will see.

~~~

"Blessed are the poor in spirit, for theirs is the kingdom of heaven. "Blessed are those who mourn, for they shall be comforted. "Blessed are the meek, for they shall inherit the earth. "Blessed are those who hunger and thirst for righteousness, for they shall be satisfied. "Blessed are the merciful, for they shall receive mercy.
Matthew 5:3-7

Blessed is he who comes in the name of the Lord! We bless you from the house of the Lord.
Psalm 118:26

Be delighted with the Lord.
Then He will give you all the desires of your heart.
Psalms 37:4

Do not be anxious about anything, but in everything by prayer and supplication with thanksgiving let your requests be made known to God.
Philippians 4:6

Therefore I tell you, whatever you ask in prayer, believe that you have received it, and it will be yours.
Mark 11:24

Michael Gasaway

In Heaven They Do Roam

She had raised him up since he was just a puppy;
Together they had roamed many a trail and he always made her
happy.

Many a tear she had shed over the years with just him by her
side;
Just one look and she could see the devotion and love in his
eyes.

Oh the many happy memories, together they had shared;
Since he was just a pup for him she had lovingly cared.

He had been her trusted companion for oh so many years;
Now he was losing life's battle and her heart was gripped with
fear.

Whether it be a dog, cat or a horse that here you have loved;
You know that they were all sent here from heaven above.

Sharing their unconditional love with you like no other;
A trusted friend by your side always, long ago you did discover.

Believing in my heart, that up in heaven they also do roam;
For without our trusted companions, it would be hard to call it
home.

They must be roaming the pastures, woods and fields up on
high;
Just passing the time away until one day again they are by your
side.

Love your pet each day that you have them here to play;
For in due time, God will also call them home to stay.

I know that the loss of a beloved pet is like losing a family
member;
The tears will fall, your heart will ache, but the happy times you'll
always remember.

So while they are here with you, give them the love they are
due;

For they have always been by your side and asked nothing of you.

Keep your mind open and cherish the memories in your heart;
It is only for a time and not forever that you will be apart.

∾∾∾

The wolf shall dwell with the lamb, and the leopard shall lie down with the young goat, and the calf and the lion and the fattened calf together; and a little child shall lead them.
Isaiah 11:6

Then I saw heaven opened, and behold, a white horse! The one sitting on it is called Faithful and True, and in righteousness he judges and makes war.
Revelation 19:11

"And all flesh shall see the salvation of God.'"
Luke 3:6

The wolf and the lamb shall graze together; the lion shall eat straw like the ox, and dust shall be the serpent's food. They shall not hurt or destroy in all my holy mountain," says the Lord.
Isaiah 65:25

Michael Gasaway

Love's Fate

Purple, lavender and pink are the colors she loves the best;
But she also loves the colors she sees with each beautiful sunset.

Alone she sits and watches as the sun fades beyond the distant
trees;
Another night alone and she wonders where her true love might
be.

She wonders, will tomorrow be the day that into her life he might
walk?
Not really looking, but with a good man it would be great to just
sit and talk.

To share life's many experiences and yes to be there when she's
blue;
Isn't that the way God had intended it to be, long ago, the
sharing of just two.

This man in her dreams she is sure that he'll make her laugh and
smile;
He may even be the one, to walk her down the aisle.

With each breath she takes, and through another lonely night she
does wait;
In her heart she knows that God has someone special, as part of
loves fate.

Don't let worry, fear and a lack of faith stop your dream from
coming true;
God gave us all free choice and what you choose to believe is up
to you.

So never give up and keep trusting and put your faith in God
above;
He will give you the desires of your heart, and bring you true
love.

~~~

Delight yourself in the Lord, and he will give you the desires of your heart. Psalm 37:4

The heart of man plans his way, but the Lord establishes his steps. Proverbs 16:9

Now faith is the assurance of things hoped for, the conviction of things not seen. Hebrews 11:1

For I know the plans I have for you, declares the Lord, plans for welfare and not for evil, to give you a future and a hope. Jeremiah 29:11

There is no fear in love, but perfect love casts out fear. For fear has to do with punishment, and whoever fears has not been perfected in love. 1 John 4:18

And let us not grow weary of doing good, for in due season we will reap, if we do not give up. Galatians 6:9

Do not be anxious about anything, but in everything by prayer and supplication with thanksgiving let your requests be made known to God. Philippians 4:6

Therefore I tell you, whatever you ask in prayer, believe that you have received it, and it will be yours. Mark 11:24

*For still the vision awaits its appointed time; it hastens to the end—it will not lie. If it seems slow, wait for it; it will surely come; it will not delay.
Habakkuk 2:3*

Time to Begin Again

In the distance she can hear and feel the thunder down in her
very soul;
Out beyond the breakers the lightning flashes across the sky
putting on such an amazing show.

Streaking all across the sky the bolts of lightning just seem to
create such an amazing sight;
Inside it stirs her in so many ways and yet brings her such
delight.

Oh how she loves to sit and watch as those thunder storms start
to rumble in;
Seems to speak to her in so many ways and yet sends tingles up
and down her skin.

It has always been that way for her, but most just don't seem to
understand;
How she has yearned to sit there and watch the show, and just
hold that one special hand.

The colors of purple, gray, orange, yellow and pink just seem to
flash all across the sky;
But sometimes in her mind she remembers and can't help but
wonder, why God why.

So alone she sits and contemplates her fate as she feels the first
soft drops of rain upon her skin;
Smiling she remembers that the sunshine and rainbows always
follow and for her, it's time to begin again.

~~~

Delight yourself in the Lord, and he will give you the desires of your heart.
Psalm 37:4

For the Lord God is a sun and shield; the Lord bestows favor and honor. No good thing does he withhold from those who walk uprightly.
Psalm 84:11

He will bring forth your righteousness as the light, and your justice as the noonday.
Psalm 37:6

Commit your way to the Lord; trust in him, and he will act.
Psalm 37:5

For still the vision awaits its appointed time; it hastens to the end—it will not lie. If it seems slow, wait for it; it will surely come; it will not delay.
Habakkuk 2:3

For everything there is a season, and a time for every matter under heaven:
Ecclesiastes 3:1

Michael Gasaway

Sometimes in Life

The guilt and resentment she tried to brush from her mind;
But the thoughts inside kept taking her back in time.

Back into her past and a very special place;
To where she had worn a real smile on her beautiful face.

Now alone she traveled this dusty trail of life;
Wondering why each day was filled with so much strife.

Some days she thought of going out and trying again;
To give it one more try and this time to win.

Her heart said yes, give it one more try;
Her mind stopped her cold as the months went by.

Sometimes in life we just have to go ahead and just begin;
You only regret the things you didn't do in the end.

Seek out God's word and His will to be done;
Then take the steps that lead your heart with the rising sun.

It's never too late in life to make things right;
Just always pray for His guidance each day and night.

There may be times you have to just let go and start anew;
God will guide your steps and always lead and direct you.

Let go of the negative things that haunt you from the past;
It's the only way you'll ever find a true love that will last.

Maybe forward God may take you or back you never know;
Just put your trust in Him and then just let go.

So into tomorrow she goes to give life and love one more try;
This time around, she'll let her heart, head and God be her guide.

As the stars shined so big and bright on that Texas night;
She once again found her true love and it felt so right.

Yes sometimes making amends and starting fresh works the
best;
Always let God be your guide and direct your steps.